LONDON CHRISTMAS

TRAVEL GUIDE

A PocketGuide Festive Holiday Charm of London: Explore,Experience, and Enjoy

MICHAEL E. HOWELL

This London Christmas Travel Guide opens a doorway into the center of holiday enchantment as you wander through its pages. London's holiday appeal is a tapestry made of the city's past, present, and future. This book serves as an explorers book guide to help you find your way through the maze of activities, attractions, and itineraries so that your Christmas journey is full of joy.

Experiences for every taste and inclination have been selected inside these pages. London's rich tapestry provides everything, be it that you're looking for the glitz of lavish celebrations or the seductive stillness of secret spaces. This guide reveals the city's seasonal attractions, seeing famous sites lit up for the holidays as well as enjoying mulled wine at little markets. Take advantage of the season's whimsy by strolling around the illuminated alleys of history. Experience the comfort of a cozy fireplace in a historic tavern or ice skate beneath the stars.

Step beyond your comfort zone to find jewels hidden from the beaten route. Let the spirit of the occasion lead you as you browse through this guide to a wonderful London Christmas. May your trip through this magical city be illuminated with experiences as colorful as the lights on the imposing Christmas tree in Trafalgar Square.

Welcome to the enchantment of Christmastime in London.

CONTENTS

LONDON OVER CHRISTMAS TIME

London becomes a winter paradise filled with celebrations and pleasure throughout the coldest months. The city dons a distinctive appearance, decked up with glistening lights, holiday accents, and a jovial atmosphere that twirls through its streets. It's a moment when history and fun collide, making historic sites even more alluring.

London around the holidays is like a fairytale come to life. Imagine taking a walk along a famous boulevard when the festive season is in full swing and the air is fresh with anticipation. The city welcomes you to partake in the celebration as it is dressed in its finest seasonal attire. There is an evident air of celebration among the historical splendor, contemporary elegance, and different cultures that coexist in this busy city. The jolly time of year engulfs everyone in its warm embrace. The city invites everyone to take part in this happy feast, regardless of being a citizen or guest. London during Christmas is a sight to see, the well-known buildings lit by a million lights and the quaint markets emitting a merry scent. With the glittering illumination, the city's crevices come alive, and the merry conversation of people provides a musical background to the sight.

CAPTIVATING CHRISTMAS ATTRACTIONS

Big Ben and the Houses of Parliament: A Christmastime Timeless Marvel

Big Ben and the Houses of Parliament, which tower majestically along the River Thames, represent the everlasting beauty of London. The Big Ben clock tower, with its enormous hands precisely recording the passing of time, is a well-known emblem of the city. Located in the heart of London, on the north bank of the River Thames. The address is: Westminster, London SW1A 0AA, United Kingdom.

The area around Big Ben and the Houses of Parliament becomes a magnificent scene as winter weaves its mesmerizing spell. The imposing building is lighted, highlighting its architectural magnificence against the winter sky's waning light. The faces of the clocks come to life with a bright light, becoming a beacon in the joyous night. The Gothic-style Houses of Parliament, which are next to the tower, have a seductive charm. The ornate elements of the stately facades, spires, and arches contrast well with the nearby modernism. The River Thames glides past, giving the setting a flowing beauty. This place turns into a hotspot of celebration around Christmas. Buildings are decked up, and the holiday spirit permeates the air.

The chimes of Big Ben are complemented by the lyrical melody of carolers as they fill the air. Both tourists and locals congregate here to photograph the enchantment and make memories in front of this everlasting wonder. This spot, tucked away in the middle of London, is more than just a famous monument. It serves as a reminder of the city's past and a lighthouse that invites everyone to experience the wonder of Christmas in an enduring environment.

Winter Wonderland in Hyde Park: A Magical Getaway at Christmas

Hyde Park, located right in the center of London; Hyde Park, London W2 2UH, United Kingdom, transforms into the lovely Winter Wonderland throughout Christmas. With this exciting event, the sizable park is transformed into a fantastical setting that welcomes everyone to explore. Hyde Park decks itself up in a dazzling array of shimmering lights and holiday accents as the winter cold sets in. Visitors are drawn into its warm embrace by the enthusiasm and pleasure that permeate the air.

The park is transformed into a work of art with vivid colors and upbeat noises, offering an escape from reality into a paradise of pleasure. When strolling through streets decorated with sparkling lights as the aroma of holiday delicacies fills the air. Laughter and upbeat conversation flood the air, spreading the festive mood. An environment of harmony and joy is created as families, friends, and strangers come together to enjoy the festivities. There is an experience waiting for every soul, the legendary Giant Observation Wheel affording a sweeping perspective of this winter paradise and the charming Christmas markets exhibiting one-of-a-kind crafts and scrumptious delights. The attractiveness is enhanced with ice skating, exhilarating rides, and enchanting performances, providing a wonderful experience for both young and elderly. Winter Wonderland at Hyde Park is a charming getaway into the wonder of the holiday season. It personifies the pleasure of the holidays and the sense of community.

Oxford Street Christmas Lights: A Gleaming Display at Christmas

During the holiday season, Oxford Street, a well-known street in the center of London, is a major shopping street located in the West End of London. Its central location and popularity make it one of the busiest shopping districts in the city. (Oxford St, London W1C 1JN, United Kingdom). It's easily accessible by public transportation, and the street is well-known for its extensive range of shops, boutiques, department stores, and eateries, making it a prime shopping destination in London.

During Christmas it takes on a stunning change. With a dazzling display of Christmas lights illuminating the night, the once-bustling street now transforms into a work of art. As dusk approaches, Oxford Street starts to sparkle, emitting a stunning show of colors and patterns. A bright canopy is formed by the many lights that have been painstakingly strung down the length of the roadway. The lights flicker and dance to an unknown beat, filling the air with a feeling of surprise and excitement. Both residents and tourists who are on foot halt to marvel at this magnificent sight. The lights, which are arranged in complex patterns and forms, provide a comforting warmth that draws people into its mesmerizing embrace. It's a visual feast that makes the heart happy and excited for the holiday season.

It's a symphony of light. One cannot help but be taken into a magical realm while passing under this magnificent canopy. The stores and boutiques along the street participate in the festivities by decking up the front of their establishments with holiday accents, enhancing the joyous ambiance. The Christmas decorations on Oxford Street are a celebration of the season. They provide a bright light on the way, leading people through the wonder of Christmas in this busy area of London.

Ice Skating at Somerset House: A Christmastime Experience to Remember

Historic landmark Somerset House, located in the City of Westminster on the Strand in the heart of London. It is widely accessible and visible from many locations across the city since it is located along the north bank of the River Thames. Somerset House, Strand, London, WC2R 1LA, United Kingdom, is the address. It is transformed into a winter wonderland throughout the holiday season.

The vast courtyard, which is often packed with activity, acquires a peaceful appeal as it transforms into a spotless ice rink, encouraging everyone to glide and twirl in this idyllic environment. As you go out onto the ice, you can feel the anticipation in the crisp air. The rink is illuminated by a gentle light show, which gives off a lovely atmosphere. The thrill of ice skating unites skaters of all ages and abilities who are there, each with their own goals and desires. A musical symphony of joy is created by the sound of blades slashing across the ice, laughing, and sporadic applause. While little youngsters take their first tentative glides to their delighted parents' joyful applause, couples skate elegantly while holding hands. It's a joyful sight that celebrates the season and the happiness it offers. The experience goes beyond ice skating when Somerset House's neoclassical architecture is present. A voyage through a classic winter story is involved. Every heart on the ice is filled with holiday cheer as the brisk air heralds the impending celebrations.

History Revealed at The Tower of London over the holidays

The Tower of London, which is located along the banks of the River Thames, is a physical reminder of the city's turbulent and colorful past. This old fortress provides a one-of-a-kind trip through time as the Christmas season approaches, a journey into the past that is filled with the echoes of bygone periods.

Picture yourself in front of the massive stone walls, which have been worn and etched by centuries of tales. The atmosphere exudes mystery as if it were hiding the secrets of the monarchs and famous people who have trod these halls in the past. History's essence is tangible and only waiting to be discovered. Visitors are taken into a world where history is happening right in front of their eyes as they enter via the centuries-old archways. The towering towers and turrets, each with a unique story to tell, are reached by cobblestone roads. With its commanding presence, the White Tower acts as a sentinel and a quiet observer of centuries of history. The festive season shines with a particular radiance against this historical backdrop. The stronghold is decorated, giving the age-old stones a touch of holiday charm. Christmas spirit and historical echoes combine to create a reverent and awe-inspiring ambiance. Christmastime at the Tower of London is a journey through history. It offers a look into the personalities and histories of people who influenced London's course. You enter this timeless tale as you go through its halls and courtyards, a contemporary explorer in a world rich with history.

CREATING MAGICAL ITINERARIES

London Christmas Itinerary: A Day of Christmas Shopping - Oxford Street and Covent Garden

Embracing the holiday spirit can be a rewarding experience in London, and setting out a day for Christmas shopping is a great way to fully embrace the joyous season. Oxford Street and Covent Garden are two popular locations for such a joyous adventure. These hopping centers provide a wide range of choices for discovering the ideal presents, accents, and delights during the holiday season.

One of London's biggest retail areas, Oxford Street, is a great place to start your day. The row of retailers, boutiques, and department stores displays a broad range of goods. The vivid displays and window decorations raise your mood as you stroll through the busy streets. Oxford Street offers a wide range of options to suit every taste and budget, in the case that you're looking for one-of-a-kind presents, celebratory clothing, or decorative décor. Go to Covent Garden next, a quaint neighborhood noted for its markets and artisanal businesses located in the West End of London, (Covent Garden, London WC2E 8RF). The ancient plaza, which offers a wide variety of handmade goods, regional crafts, and aesthetic treasures, is teeming with life and creativity. Finding unique presents that capture the spirit of the holiday season by exploring the market's hidden corners is in and of itself an experience.

Take some time throughout your shopping adventures to enjoy the festive atmosphere. Visitors are often serenaded by street performers and musicians, providing a colorful background for your day. During your shopping excursion, treat yourself to a hot cup of cocoa or maybe a freshly made pastry from one of the charming cafés dotted around Covent Garden. You can do your holiday shopping on Oxford Street and Covent Garden in one day, and you'll also get to experience the bustle of London at this time of year. The festive decorations, happy shoppers, and variety of offers perfectly capture the spirit of Christmas in this energetic metropolis. So get into the holiday mood, indulge in some retail therapy, and savor the happy memories you make along the way.

Itinerary for Christmas in London: A Night of Festive Delights with Mulled Wine

During the Christmas season, London has a magical allure when the sun sets and the city lights come on. A lovely way to get into the holiday spirit is to plan an evening filled with merrymaking, Christmas markets, and the comforting embrace of mulled wine.

Set off on your quest as the sky changes to twilight-colored colors. Navigate to one of the city's many colorful Christmas markets. These markets beckon with a variety of festive knickknacks, traditional crafts, and delicious seasonal foods. They are decorated with dazzling lights and vibrant booths. Listed down is a list of well-liked Christmas markets in London that are ideal for getting into the holiday spirit:

❖ **Winter Wonderland Market (Hyde Park)**

The Winter Wonderland Market, which is located in Hyde Park, transforms into a vivid kaleidoscope of activities throughout the Christmas season. As soon as you enter this wonderful realm, the air is filled with the aroma of mouthwatering food and the sound of joyful laughing. It's a symphony of joy that envelops you in the spirit of the season.

This magical bazaar unfolds like a real-life picture book. Each corner is decorated with dazzling lights and seasonal accents, creating a beautiful sight against the night sky. Each of the market's vendors offers a treasure trove of festive treats. Offerings include cozy winter clothing and handmade decorations to satisfy every need for the ideal holiday keepsake. Your senses are awoken as you go through the market by the aromas of roasted chestnuts, freshly baked pastries, and regional specialties. As tourists experience the variety of attractions, exhilarating rides along with exquisite carousels, laughter, and excitement fill the air, creating an atmosphere of unbridled delight. There is a mix of joy and nostalgia in the air. Families, friends, and strangers gather to celebrate the holiday spirit. While riding the carousel, kids are laughing and their faces are beaming with joy. Hand in hand, couples spend sweet moments in front of the dazzling lights, making lifelong memories.

Hyde Park's Winter Wonderland Market offers an unforgettable experience. It's a celebration of the time of year and a tribute to happiness and community. The memories made here are woven into the fabric of the holiday season and serve as a constant reminder of the love and enchantment that Christmas offers. It is a location where both young and old can enjoy the magic of the holidays.

❖ Southbank Centre Winter Market

The Southbank Centre Winter Market, tucked away along the banks of the River Thames, comes to life throughout the Christmas season as a vivid tapestry of seasonal festivities. The perfume of Christmas treats and the sounds of laughter fill the air as twilight falls, luring everyone inside to celebrate the season. This market is a hive of activity, a sight of sparkling lights and jovial conversation.

Along the riverfront are stands that display a variety of presents, handmade items, and delicious foods. You are welcomed as you stroll through this joyous carnival by the jubilant tunes of street musicians and the vivacious conversation of guests. Families and friends congregate to check out the market's products, and a sense of community and camaraderie permeates the scene. Children are awestruck by the creative installations and seasonal souvenirs, and their expressions are filled with amazement. Walking hand in hand, couples take in the beauty of the surroundings. The market's gourmet pleasures beckon among the holiday revelry. Warm mulled wine, freshly made cookies, and savory delights fill the air with their aromas. The food stands provide a variety of exotic delicacies, appealing to all palates and enhancing the vibrant atmosphere. The Southbank Centre Winter Market is an occasion to celebrate happiness and custom. It's a location where the Christmas spirit comes to life and the tranquility of the season is reflected in the river's calm flow. It's a beloved location for soaking up London's holiday spirit since it's a hideaway where memories are created and the sense of togetherness is appreciated.

❖ **Greenwich Market**

The quaint Greenwich Market, located in the neighborhood of Greenwich, comes alive with holiday cheer throughout the Christmas season. This market, which is tucked away among old alleyways, comes to life with a kaleidoscope of hues, aromas, and noises, giving off a genuine festive vibe. The market is a vibrant hub of tradition and innovation. A variety of handmade items, artisanal crafts, and seasonal delights are displayed at stalls that are decked up in dazzling lights and festive accents. Each vendor invites customers to explore and find the ideal Christmas gifts by presenting a special product that reflects their passion and ingenuity.

Freshly baked items with seasonal scents are permeating the market as you go through it. A melodic background is created by laughter and happy talks, reflecting the upbeat atmosphere. Couples, friends, and families with kids stroll around the booths as their faces are lighted up with anticipation. Christmastime at Greenwich Market is characterized by a strong feeling of neighborhood. The warmth of the celebrations is enhanced by the visitors' tales and smiles. The air is often filled with music and carolers, giving the area a lyrical vibe. It's a location where new traditions and old ones coexist together, and where there is a constant sense of thankfulness and generosity in every neighborhood. The market's bright energy invites you to explore and enjoy the season among the holiday cheer. Christmas at Greenwich Market is spectacular, and the memories made here are not only about the presents; they are also about the experience, the joy, and the shared moments.

❖ **The Leicester Square Holiday Market**

This market changes into a bustling and exuberant celebration of the yuletide spirit as the city decks itself up in holiday brightness. A wide variety of booths, each decked with cheerful lights and endearing accents, bring the market to life. These booths provide a charming assortment of handmade decorations, tasty sweets, and one-of-a-kind items, making them a treasure trove for those looking for the ideal gift for their loved ones. You are surrounded by the joyous atmosphere as you stroll around the market. The air is filled with pleasure, laughter, and the gentle melody of holiday music. People of all ages enjoy the festive mood. Their grins convey the delight of the occasion. Warm mulled wine, cinnamon, and roasted chestnuts are a pleasant scent combination that permeates the market. The alluring aromas entice you to indulge in the festive delights. It is a sensory experience that blends taste and heritage.

The tall Ferris wheel stands out as a famous landmark among the busy market. It gives the celebrations a hint of enchantment when lit up in vivid colors. The market is an event that celebrates community and the spirit of giving and captures the real meaning of Christmas. The holiday spirit of the city is evident at the Leicester Square Holiday Market during Christmas. It's a location where the holiday spirit comes alive in London and everyone is welcome to join in the joyful festivities.

❖ Borough Market

Borough Market, a center for gastronomic and cultural experiences located in the Borough area of Southwark, Central London, comes alive with holiday charm throughout the Christmas season. This crowded market turns into a sanctuary for people looking for the coziness and charm of the festive season since it is tucked away among old buildings.

The market becomes a lively sight as it is decked with blinking lights and holiday accents. Stalls give a chance to savor the tastes of the season while surrounded by a wide variety of gourmet foods and festive goodies. The welcoming scent of freshly baked products and the luscious flavor of spices permeate the air, sharpening the senses. Locals and tourists congregate to participate in the holiday celebrations amidst the bustling environment. As they investigate the many options, laughing and conversation fill the air. Christmastime at Borough

Market is a sensory extravaganza. Both the flavor of the delectable holiday fare and the visual display of the culinary artistry are pleasing to the palette and the eyes. It's more than simply a market; it's an occasion to celebrate cuisine, community, and traditions while embracing the spirit of the holiday season. This market, situated in London's historic Borough neighborhood, perfectly captures the spirit of Christmas. It's a location where a treasured memory is created for everyone who enters this festive environment thanks to the harmonic union of a love of cuisine and the pleasure of the holiday season..

❖ Columbia Road Flower Market

The vibrant Columbia Road Flower Market, a growing treasure that thrives with charm, particularly during the holiday season, is situated in the center of London's East End. This lively market, which is tucked away among old buildings, transforms into a magical tapestry of hues and fragrances throughout the holiday. The market wakes with a riot of colors as the air welcomes the crisp December wind. The cheery wreaths and vibrant flowers combine to form a kaleidoscope, a visual composition that captures the essence of the holiday. The normally busy cobblestone route suddenly becomes a scented oasis of seasonal happiness.

Visitors are invited to see for themselves the natural beauty of stalls that are decorated with seasonal flowers and foliage. The air is filled with the perfume of pine, cinnamon, and other seasonal scents, taking the senses on an exquisite voyage. The market is bustling with shoppers carrying bunches of colorful flowers, their banter and laughing bringing happiness to the area. Street entertainers and musicians contribute to the celebratory atmosphere while serenading the throng among the floral splendor. Families, friends, and plant lovers congregate to take advantage of this special market experience, creating lasting memories and spreading the pleasure of the season. Christmastime at the Columbia Road Flower Market is a celebration of nature's splendor. It's a natural place where flowers are included in the seasonal celebrations and the brilliant colors reflect the joy of the occasion. It is a well-liked location for those looking for the charm and perfume of Christmas in full bloom, and it is situated in the Bethnal Green neighborhood of London.

❖ **Camden Market**

The renowned Camden Market, a dynamic tapestry of innovation and culture. This market changes into a vibrant spectacle throughout the holiday, reflecting the true spirit of Christmas. The market is a busy place with booths brimming with an unusual selection of presents, handmade items, and one-of-a-kind treasures. Every crevice and nook is a riot of color and imagination. Street merchants advertise their goods, luring guests to explore and find unique discoveries. As you stroll through this center of holiday activity, you are surrounded by a happy mood. An atmosphere of sheer joy is created by the sound of laughing, the flavors of street cuisine, and the sight of happy people. Everywhere in the world, groups of friends, families, and guests get together to enjoy the holiday. A musical symphony is added to the joyous atmosphere as musicians and artists take center stage among the happy mayhem. Artists demonstrate their skills and captivate the audience with their creativity. A perfect fusion of tradition and contemporary, it's a celebration of creativity and community.

These markets provide a delightful and lively atmosphere that is excellent for soaking up the festive mood and discovering the best presents for your loved ones.

As the night falls, make your way to a little corner where mulled wine, a traditional winter drink, is waiting. Allow the warm, comforting perfume of the red wine and spice combination to fill your senses. Feel the spirit of the season beginning to burn inside you as you sip this festive elixir and let the flavors dance on your palette. The evenings of holiday treats, which includes visiting Christmas markets and indulging in mulled wine, gives a surreal tour of London's winter wonderland. A memory that captures the genuine spirit of the festive season is made when lively marketplaces and the cozy embrace of mulled wine come together. It's a night to remember because it's when the Christmas spirit comes alive in the center of the city.

Warm Up Your Christmas Spirit: Where to Enjoy Mulled Wine in London

Finding quaint locations in London where you can enjoy mulled wine during the merry Christmas season is suggested here. Finding a cozy area to partake of this particular beverage will enhance the pleasure and happiness of the festive season.

❖ Traditional Pubs

Traditional pubs in London are quaint, vintage bars that at times offer a warm, friendly atmosphere. These bars still have traditional furnishings and décor, which exudes a feeling of tradition and neighborhood. They serve as gathering spots where people congregate to partake of a range of libations, mingle, and experience London's real pub culture. Down is a list of traditional pubs in London where you can enjoy mulled wine during the festive Christmas season:

- **Ye Olde Cheshire Cheese:**

Ye Olde Cheshire Cheese, situated in 145 Fleet Street, London, is a symbol of heritage and custom. This quaint business, with its centuries-old attractiveness, transforms into a quintessential destination for people seeking the true spirit of Christmas when the holiday season blesses the city. You are thrust into the past as soon as you enter Ye Olde Cheshire Cheese. Warm light emanating from the flickering glimmer of antique lanterns reveals the interior's rustic wooden beams and ancient charm. It's a location where happy talks from today coexist with whispers from the past.

Christmastime sees that the pub's ambiance changes into a warm haven. Customers are encouraged to assemble and exchange seasonal tales in front of the roaring fireplace, which provides a cozy embrace against the winter cold. You are immersed in a lovely sensory experience as the aroma of spiced mulled wine and traditional food fills the air. There is a mix of fun and friendship in the air. Locals and foreigners alike get together to enjoy the holidays. A contagious excitement flows from one table to the next as laughter and gladness resound throughout the space.

- **George Inn:**

The venerable George Inn is a timeless sanctuary in 75-77 Borough High Street, that takes on a unique attraction during the Christmas season. This centuries-old restaurant, tucked away in the middle of the city's busy streets, calls with a taste of both tradition and celebration. When you enter the George Inn, a world of old-world elegance greets you. The quaint nooks, old brickwork, and wooden beams all contribute to the comfortable ambiance. It's a setting where the history's echoes through the walls beckon you to celebrate the season. The inn decks itself up in a festive shroud over the holiday season. Warmthening golden lights shine, illuminating the historic interior. The roaring fireplace becomes the center of attention, giving off a cozy and nostalgic vibe. The alluring perfume of seasonal treats permeates the air, titillating the senses. As customers congregate, a sense of community emerges. The air is filled with laughter and chat, which adds another element of coziness to the setting. During the holidays, The George Inn transforms into a gathering place where tales are told and new memories are created.

- **The Lamb and Flag:**

The Lamb and Flag pub, located at 33 Rose Street, shines with warmth and joy throughout the holiday. This pleasant restaurant, which offers a beautiful mix of tradition and seasonal pleasure, is tucked away among the old streets. As soon as you enter The Lamb and Flag, you are welcomed with a warm hug. The traditional timber interiors, embellished with delicate lighting and festive accents, provide a warm and welcoming atmosphere. It's a location where the festive spirit of the time of year combines well with the traditional pub charm. The tavern morphs into a festive scene during Christmas. The historic elements are illuminated by soft lights that glitter. Warmth and nostalgia are emitted by the roaring fireplace. The air is filled with the delicious aroma of seasonal food, tempting the senses and enhancing the joyful mood. As customers congregate, a sense of community emerges. The atmosphere is filled with laughter and conversations that help people form friendships and share experiences. The Lamb and Flag offers a peek of London's holiday cheer. Its central position in the busy metropolis enables both residents and visitors to fully experience the enchanted Christmas atmosphere. It's a call to enjoy the season, one drink and one belly laugh at a time.

- **The Churchill Arms:**

The Churchill Arms in 119 Kensington Church Street, London, is a magnificent sight, particularly during the holidays. This famous bar, that embodies a combination of history and joyful enthusiasm, is hidden among the busy streets. You enter The Churchill Arms and enter a magical realm. The outside has been transformed into a visual joy with a plethora of dazzling lights and holiday accents. It's a setting where the spirit of the season blends with the enduring allure of the pub. The Churchill Arms transforms magically throughout the holiday season. The lights provide a spellbinding spectacle that illuminates the surroundings and the façade. The warm interior is decorated with holiday accents, providing the ideal environment for the festivities of the time of year.

A delicious fusion of spiced mulled wine and regional food will be detected in the air. As customers assemble to enjoy the festivities, the atmosphere is filled with a symphony of talk and laughing. The Churchill Arms offers a peek of London's holiday cheer. Its central position in the busy metropolis enables both residents and visitors to fully experience the enchanted Christmas atmosphere. It's a call to enjoy the joy of the season, one drink and a grin at a time.

- **The Mayflower Pub**

Located by the Thames, the Mayflower Pub is a timeless haven at 117 Rotherhithe Street, London. This old bar, which combines history and seasonal pleasure, beckons from its secluded location along the riverside. You enter The Mayflower Pub and enter a world of longing for ships. The hardwood interior, which is embellished with tasteful accents and subdued lighting, radiates a warm and inviting atmosphere. It's a location where the timeless appeal of the bar coexists with the season's good humor.

The Mayflower Pub dresses festively at Christmas time. A calming glow from the lights gives off a welcoming atmosphere. The cozy ambiance is enhanced by the flickering candles and the roaring fire. The air is enticingly scented with seasonal treats, tickling the senses. The atmosphere is festive as customers congregate. A happy mood is created by the harmonic blending of conversations and laughing. Christmastime transforms the Mayflower

Pub into more than just a bar; it becomes a gathering place for friends and family to bond. The Mayflower Pub offers a peek of London's Christmas atmosphere. Due to its proximity to the Thames, both residents and guests can enjoy the enchanted holiday atmosphere. It's a call to enjoy the season, one drink, and good company at a time.

- **The Ten Bells:**

The Ten Bells is a historic tavern located in the East End of London at 84 Commercial Street, that has a unique appeal, particularly during the holidays. This charming business, that offers a beautiful mix of tradition and Christmas celebration, calls from among the bustling streets. You enter The Ten Bells and find yourself in a realm of enduring enchantment. The charming interior, which is decorated with antique touches and gentle lighting, has a cozy and welcoming atmosphere. It's a location where the timeless appeal of the bar and the excitement of the season smoothly converge. The Ten Bells decks itself up in festive magnificence over the holiday season. A cozy and pleasant atmosphere is created by the twinkling of soft lights. The roaring fire, which exudes both warmth and nostalgia, becomes the center of attention. The air is filled with the delicious aroma of seasonal treats, tempting the senses. As customers congregate, a sense of community emerges. There is an atmosphere of shared enjoyment in the air as conversations and laughter reverberate. The Ten Bells is a gathering place where relationships are valued and memories are created.

The Ten Bells gives viewers a taste of the joyous atmosphere that permeates London's East End. Its location in the bustling area enables both residents and guests to fully experience the enchanted Christmas atmosphere. The season is being invited to be savored, one drink and one shared moment at a time.

- **The Anchor Bankside:**

Situated near the Globe Theatre. The Anchor Bankside is a place of warmth and celebration right in the middle of London at 34 Park Street. This old tavern, which is tucked away next to the River Thames, beckons with its appealing combination of festive fun and tradition. You feel a warm hug as you enter The Anchor Bankside. The hardwood inside is decorated with glistening lights and festive accents to create a warm and welcoming ambiance. It's a location where the festive spirit of the season mingles well with the nautical beauty of the bar.

The Anchor Bankside is transformed into a mystical refuge throughout the holidays. The historic characteristics are highlighted by the delicate glow that the soft lights reflect. Warmth and a feeling of reminiscence are given out by the crackling fireplace. The air is filled with the delicious scent of holiday food, tempting the senses and enhancing the festive mood. The atmosphere of celebration and community is heightened when customers congregate. The air is filled with laughing and conversation, making it a happy environment. A center of festive joy where memories are spun and shared. The Anchor Bankside gives visitors a taste of London's holiday cheer. Its proximity to the Thames enables both residents and guests to fully experience the enchanted holiday atmosphere.

These traditional pubs in London offer a taste of Christmas through their mulled wine offerings, inviting you to experience the warmth and joy of the holiday season.

Santa's Grottos & Christmas Shows in London during Christmas: A Family-Friendly Adventure

London becomes a mystical paradise around Christmas, particularly for families seeking the pleasure of the season. A fun approach to making enduring memories and celebrating the holiday season with loved ones is to go on a family-friendly tour via Santa's Grottos and Christmas plays.

Day 1.Morning

Visit one of London's magical Santa's Grottos to start your experience. Visit the renowned Hamleys, a toy shop with exquisite holiday decorations and a grotto where kids can see Santa Claus. Observe the joy in your children's eyes as they express their desires to Santa in this enchanted environment.

Visit a neighborhood eatery or café for a comfortable family meal. Enjoy substantial lunches and classic Christmas goodies to re energize for the remainder of the day.

Afternoon:

Head to Covent Garden, where lively acts fill the streets. Be amazed by the excitement that street performers and artists bring to the holiday season with their performances.

Evening:

Cap off the day with a touching Christmas performance. Get theater tickets for a show that the whole family can enjoy, like "The Snowman" or "A Christmas Carol." Enjoy the spellbinding tale and amazing performances, and then leave the theater with your hearts full of festive cheer.

Day 2.Morning:

Go to a famous Santa's Grotto in London, such as Harrods. Allow your kids to enjoy the breathtaking decor and magical Santa experiences. Record those priceless moments when they get a tiny gift and exchange holiday greetings. Indulge in a joyous meal at a neighborhood restaurant while taking in the Christmas-themed décor and specialties that capture the essence of the season.

Afternoon:

Go to the joyous amusement park Winter Wonderland in Hyde Park. Enjoy the fun of family-friendly attractions, games, and rides. Don't miss Santa Land, where children can engage in fun activities and re-meet Santa Claus.

Evening:

Finish your journey with a captivating tour of Christmas lights. Explore Oxford Street, Regent Street, and Carnaby Street, where the night is illuminated by spectacular lights and festive decorations. Observe the awe and delight on your children's faces as they take in the enchanted display of Christmas lights in London.

This family-friendly tour of London's Santa's Grottos, holiday performances, and seasonal attractions guarantees fun times and priceless memories. Make this Christmas a wonderful one by getting into the festive mood with your loved ones.

Christmas carols and church services in London: A Calm Evening

Through quiet nights filled with Christmas songs and church services, London, with its rich history and different customs, provides a pleasant and tranquil opportunity to appreciate the genuine spirit of Christmas. It's an event that captures the holiday spirit and provides a moment of delight and meditation.

Day 1: Getting Ready for the Evening

Prepare your hearts and thoughts for the spiritual adventure that lies ahead before beginning your tranquil evening. Visit one of London's stunning parks, such as Hyde Park or St. James's Park, for a stroll. Allow the tranquility of the evening to prepare you via nature and fresh air. Enjoy a quick lunch at a neighboring café. Use this time to unwind and reflect as you prepare for the evening ahead.

Late in the afternoon:

Visit a historic church in London known for hosting lovely Christmas carol sessions. During the holidays, Westminster Abbey and St. Paul's Cathedral often offer beautiful carol services. To get a good seat and see the majesty of these beautiful cathedrals, get there early. The stately Westminster Abbey, located in 20 Dean's Yard, London, serves as a timeless symbol of the city's history and spirituality, particularly during the Christmas holiday. For visitors looking to experience the actual spirit of the holiday, its breathtaking Gothic architecture and centuries-old resonance make it an intriguing location.

You are welcomed by the splendor of Westminster Abbey's towering arches and magnificent stained glass windows as you enter. Awe and respect are evoked by the immensity of the nave and the interior's meticulous embellishments. During Christmas, this revered location, where British kings are crowned and history is made, transforms into a haven of tranquility and introspection. Westminster Abbey is filled with the melodic notes of traditional songs throughout this holy season, as choirs sing in perfect harmony. The candlelight rituals give the old stones a soft glow that gives off an otherworldly atmosphere. The nativity scenes and Christmas decorations heighten the celebration and reflect the enthusiasm of the occasion. Christmastime visits to Westminster Abbey are both spiritual and historical journeys. The setting, among London's famous monuments, provides a window into the city's rich history. It's an invitation to enjoy the holiness and peace of Christmas while being graced by custom and the echoes of time.

St. Paul's Cathedral, which is eminently in St Paul's Churchyard, epitomizes classic elegance, particularly during the holiday season of Christmas. Those looking to experience the actual essence of the occasion will find it to be a mesmerizing location because of its spectacular dome and historical importance. When you approach St. Paul's

Cathedral, its imposing façade and recognizable dome that dominates the London skyline will welcome you. You are invited into a sacred space by the elaborate architectural elements and the atmosphere of solemnity. During Christmas, this holy place, where historical events have been inscribed, is transformed into a refuge of tranquility and devotion. The inside of St. Paul's Cathedral is transformed into a symphony of hymns and songs throughout this holy season. The choir's singing fills the cathedral's void with songs that ring forth the festive spirit of Christmas. Candlelight casts a soothing glow over the elaborate building, evoking a peaceful and spiritual atmosphere.

Christmastime visits to St. Paul's Cathedral are not only spiritual journeys but also journeys through history and architectural styles. The setting, in the middle of the busy metropolis, provides a window into London's rich history. It's an invitation to embrace the holiness and grace of Christmas while being surrounded by historical echoes and the festive mood.

Day Two: Getting into the Christmas Spirit

To buy a candle or two, go to your neighborhood market or small store. A candle will serve as a sign of peace and optimism during a religious service. Select scented candles that speak to you and your family. Get there to attend the evening's carol service at the designated church. A really lovely and tranquil ambiance is created by the gentle glow of candles, the musical songs, and the feeling of fellowship. Let the holiday cheer that emanates from the songs flood your heart and elevate your spirits. Enjoy a nice meal at a neighboring restaurant or café after the service. By discussing your thoughts and favorite moments from the carol service, you can promote harmony and unity.

Early Evening:

Take a minute to yourself as the day comes to a close to consider what Christmas is all about. Allow the spirit of the season to surround you, be that it is via prayer, a sincere conversation, or a calm stroll.

Enjoy the grandeur of London's church services and songs as you embrace the calmness and serenity of Christmas. Your heart and soul will feel comforted and at peace as a result of this subtle reminder of the happiness and love that characterize this unique time of year.

EXCITING THINGS TO DO THIS CHRISTMAS

Walking the Festive Streets: Street Performances and the Joyful Spirit of Christmas in London

Christmas in London is a lovely time of year, with the streets filled with revelers and holiday cheer. The variety of street acts that beautify the city during this joyous time is one of the lovely features of it, filling the air with happy music and enhancing the festive mood.

Observing the Public Displays:

You'll come across a ton of street performers as you stroll through London's busy streets around Christmas. These performers, vivacious musicians along with talented dancers and cheery carolers, add to the vibrant and happy mood of the city.

The Covent Garden

Start your journey at Covent Garden, a location famous for its energetic street acts. Admire the numerous performers showing their skills among the streets that have been decorated for the holiday. The vibrant atmosphere and infectious enthusiasm here provide the ideal mood for your adventure.

The Southbank Center

You might see a variety of street acts over the holiday season at the Southbank Centre, another energetic spot situated at Belvedere Road. Get involved with the creative and talented artists who are enhancing the joyful environment.

Leicester Square

Visit Leicester Square, a bustling center that is home to a profusion of street performers throughout the holiday season, to continue your tour. These performers use the lively plaza as a stage, enthralling the crowd with their dexterous performances and enhancing the holiday spirit.

Markets for Christmas

Street performers are seen at several of London's Christmas markets, including Winter Wonderland in Hyde Park and the Christmas Market at Southbank Centre. These markets are a must-visit throughout the season because they provide a beautiful combination of celebrations, shopping, and street entertainment.

Oxford Street and Regent Street

You can come across unexpected yet enjoyable street acts as you travel along the renowned retail districts of Regent Street and Oxford Street. These vivacious performances often astound and delight both customers and guests, bringing the pleasure of Christmas into the air.

The magic of Christmas in London is not only in its well-known monuments but also in the bustling streets that come alive with the skills and fervor of street performers. Engage with these performers, be enthralled by their performances, and let the festive ambiance fill your heart with the real spirit of the season. You will come away from it with priceless memories and a heart full of festive pleasure. It is a tour through the joyful essence of London.

Enjoying Holiday Snacks During Christmas in London

Christmas in London is a season of pleasure, indulgence, and celebration, especially when it comes to the mouthwatering selection of holiday sweets. With an explosion of aromas and gastronomic pleasures that entice taste buds and warm hearts, the city celebrates the festive season. During this lovely time of the year, there is something to fulfill every taste, time-honored classics and cutting-edge inventions.

❖ **Christmas Markets Exploration: A Gastronomic Adventure**

The Christmas markets in London are a veritable treasure trove of holiday goodies. Wander through the light-up, wooden chalets where the fragrance of smoky sausages, roasted chestnuts, and warm, spiced cider fills the air. These markets provide a wonderful selection of traditional foods that are an essential component of the Christmas season. During Christmas, Hyde Park's Winter Wonderland is a gourmet paradise. The choices are bratwurst as well as crêpes and hot chocolate with marshmallows. Enjoy festive fudges, gingerbread cookies, and roasted almonds. While you explore the magical celebrations, the sweet and savory delicacies provide a nice break. You can enjoy a variety of foreign and British goodies at the Southbank Centre's Christmas Market. Enjoy a selection of foreign food, delicious mince pies, and toasty roasted chestnuts. This is a location that every food aficionado must check out because of the happy environment and delectable delicacies.

Classical British Delights: Adopting the Traditions

- **Dessert for Christmas:**

Christmas pudding is a decadent, fruity dessert that is cooked to perfection and is a traditional Christmas treat. It is a representation of the holiday season when served with brandy sauce or clotted cream.

- **Mince pies:**

Christmastime isn't complete without mince pies, which have a spiced fruit filling enveloped in buttery pastry. They are a wonderful delicacy that captures the tastes of the season and can be enjoyed warm or cold.

- **Turkey and trimmings for roasting:**

A delicious roast turkey is a common centerpiece of a Christmas meal in London. It's a classic and hearty pleasure served with stuffing, roast potatoes, Brussels sprouts, and cranberry sauce.

Savoring the New: Modern Twists & Culinary Innovations

- **Cocktails with a holiday theme:**

Throughout the holiday season, London's clubs and pubs create distinctive drinks with festive themes.

You may celebrate the holidays in style with hot cocoa, spiced cider, mulled wine, and seasonal martinis that have been expertly crafted.

- **Desserts Inspired by Christmas:**

Modern bakeries and patisseries in London come up with inventive holiday sweets. To explore the creative side of Christmas goodies, try gingerbread-flavored macarons, yule log cakes, or even biscuits in the form of Christmas trees.

Consuming holiday sweets around Christmas in London is about making sweet memories with loved ones. Every taste is a reminder of the happiness and coziness that come with the Christmas season, be it that you want to stick with the traditional or embrace the new. Let the holiday scents of Christmas in London dance on your taste receptors and stay in your heart long after the holiday has passed.

Shopping for Special Christmas Gifts at London's Artisan Markets and Boutique Stores

What better way to celebrate the season of giving and receiving in London than by choosing special presents for your loved ones? London has a wide range of possibilities for shopping, including charming boutique shops and bustling artisan markets, where you will be able to buy unique gifts with a personalized touch.

Visit the London artisan markets to see where creativity abounds. Skilled craftsmen and craftspeople may be found in many markets, including Greenwich Market and Borough Market. You will see for yourself artisanal cuisine, handmade jewelry, custom apparel, and much more here. Each piece conveys a tale of meticulous workmanship, making your present genuinely one-of-a-kind. Here are more Christmastime artisan markets in London:

- **Crafty Fox Market**

For the most recent information on the market's present location and forthcoming activities, it's a good idea to visit their official website or social media. The market often moves to various locations across the city. Crafty Fox Market is well recognized for its pop-up events, which feature independent artists and craftsmen and provide guests with a fun and constantly changing experience.

Christmastime at London's Crafty Fox Market is a thriving exhibition of artistic talent. A remarkable group of manufacturers and artists get together to exhibit their finest creations, giving the Christmas season a special touch. Visitors are drawn to the market's contagious enthusiasm and eagerness to peruse the wide variety of artisan items. You are welcomed by a variety of booths filled with a variety of handcrafted goods as soon as you arrive. The artistry on show, from exquisitely woven fabrics and carefully created jewelry, is breathtaking. A mix of fragrances, scented candles as well as freshly brewed drinks, flood the air and add to the celebratory atmosphere. Getting to know the artists is a unique experience. Each artist passionately reveals the background of their work, providing a window into their creative process. Visitors and makers bond through a common admiration for creation, fostering a spirit of friendship that permeates the environment and encourages conversation.

You will find a wide variety of presents to fit every taste as you browse the market. There is a wide range, you will see quirky and unusual along with exquisite and classic. There is something for everyone, be it that you're looking for a little trinket or a spectacular piece. The sincere friendliness and excitement of the craftsmen are what distinguish Crafty Fox Market. They dedicate themselves wholeheartedly to their work, and it shows in every item they produce. When you leave Crafty Fox Market, you don't only take the presents you bought; you also take a piece of the creative scene with you. It's an encounter that sticks with you and serves as a reminder of the wonder that happens when creativity takes center stage.

- **Old Spitalfields Market**

Old Spitalfields Market welcomes designers and artists, giving them a venue to display their works. Old Spitalfields Market in London emerges as a bustling center of seasonal cheer throughout the holiday season. This ancient market, which is located right at 16 Horner Square, emanates an alluring ambiance that draws both residents and tourists looking to experience the true spirit of Christmas. You get entranced by the wonderful market atmosphere as you get closer. The market's historic wrought-iron canopy, which rises tall, is a testimony to its past. A mix of aromas, freshly baked goods as well as evergreen wreaths, flood the air and create a warm environment. Christmastime sees the market morph into a cornucopia of unusual presents and festive treats. A variety of handcrafted items, original works of art, and delicious holiday delicacies are shown by artisans and retailers. You are enticed to experience all the skill and ingenuity exhibited by the vendors' vibrant decorations. As you browse the market, you'll find a diverse selection of goods. The booths are decorated with handcrafted ornaments, warm winter clothing, and seasonal accents. The market turns into a refuge for those looking for unique, unusual presents for their loved ones.

Additionally, the friendly exchanges with the craftspeople give the encounter a more intimate feel. Each artist recounts their creative journey with enthusiasm, bringing life to the works they have painstakingly created. A neighborhood is waking up and appreciating artistry and innovation. Old Spitalfields Market is an immersive experience that captures the spirit of Christmas; it is more than just a place to buy. The market is a place where the charm of the season comes alive thanks to the happy talk, the jolly decorations, and the merry hum. It's a celebration of individuality and group cohesiveness that leaves guests with fond memories of a joyous London.

- **Christmas in London Bridge City by the River**

Christmas at London Bridge City by the River emerges as a lovely festival over the holiday season. This quaint location, which is tucked away by the River Thames, is lit up with soft winter lights, enjoying the festive spirit. With a kaleidoscope of noises and sweet fragrances, the riverfront comes to life. The fragrance of holiday treats fills the air, while music and jovial laughter liven up the atmosphere. Awe and excitement are sparked by the sight of the imaginatively adorned booths and sparkling lights along the riverbanks. Families and friends gather here in anticipation of exploring the seasonal offers. The booths provide an extensive selection of one-of-a-kind presents, handmade decorations and delicious delicacies. A spirit of togetherness and creativity permeates the market as artisans excitedly showcase their works. The enchantment of the encounter is enhanced by the background of famous London sites. The Shard reflects the vivid holiday hues as the Tower Bridge rises tall and is decked with alluring lights. The river reflects the lights, producing a captivating spectacle that amplifies the festive mood. Additionally, the mood of joy spreads easily. People join together, strangers smiling warmly at one other as they connect through a love of the holiday season. This is a wonderful site during Christmastime because of the air's pervasive feeling of community and delight.

Christmas in London Bridge City by the River is a magical way to celebrate the season. The combination of Christmas-related sights, sounds, and smells produces an engrossing experience that leaves you with lovely memories and a heart full of the holiday spirit.

- **Camden Market**

Camden Market in London changes into a vibrant and exuberant paradise throughout the Christmas season, embracing the holiday spirit. This busy market, which is known for its unique selections and is situated in the lively Camden district at 32 Camden Lock Place, radiates an additional layer of charm during the Christmas season.

The sweet perfume of freshly baked products mixes with the earthy tones of handmade items, filling the air with a wonderful combination of aromas. Brightly decorated stalls entice customers to peruse their selection of unusual goods. Each booth offers a variety of colors and textures, making it a visual feast. You will find a wide variety of goods when exploring the market, homemade decorations and antique clothing. Craftspeople and retailers proudly display their items and are ready to tell the tales behind them. Laughter and discussion contribute to the vivacious atmosphere's happy hum. Camden Market has a distinct personality and a festive bohemian vibe that makes it stand out throughout the Christmas season. The throng is entertained by street entertainers, which enhances the carnival-like atmosphere. The market transforms into a center for expression and creativity where you can buy unique products that capture the spirit of Camden's creative community. In Camden Market, which is surrounded by the neighborhood's renowned alternative culture, inventiveness has no boundaries. Christmastime sees it converted into a center for joyous shopping and festive festivities, capturing the essence of the occasion colorfully and distinctively.

BOUTIQUE SHOPS: A LOOK AT ELEGANCE

- **Fortnum & Mason**

When Fortnum & Mason is decorated for the holidays, it seems like entering a world of festive luxury. This legendary business, located at 181 Piccadilly, adorns Piccadilly with its enduring attractiveness. The festive season highlights its historic presence. The building's outside radiates a traditional appeal, and when you go inside, lavish displays mesmerize you. The lavish interiors, which are decorated for the holidays, contribute to the festive mood. Everywhere you turn, you'll see expertly presented seasonal treats that are the height of festive pleasure. Christmastime at Fortnum & Mason is a magical display of presents, hampers, and ornaments. The tasteful selection of products, including excellent teas and delicious treats, entices the discriminating buyer.

It is a treat for those looking for the ideal Christmas gift since every shelf and nook offers treasures just waiting to be found. The shop is filled with holiday cheer, and the devoted staff makes the experience even more welcoming. Their expertise and eagerness to help make shopping a pleasurable experience. A symphony of celebration is created by the rustling of beautiful packaging and the murmur of anticipation. Also, the atmosphere is a fusion of heritage and contemporary. It's a place where you can enjoy both the traditional Christmas shopping traditions and the modern updates to the merchandise. Fortnum & Mason is a popular holiday destination for both Londoners and tourists because it personifies the pleasure of the season and the spirit of giving.

- **Liberty London:**

Liberty, the pinnacle of grace and elegance, is located right at Regent Street, tucked away among the busy streets. This exclusive department store changes into a mesmerizing fantasy throughout the holiday season. The structure itself, a masterpiece of Tudor architecture, serves as a symbol of heritage and allure. As you get closer, you're drawn in by the magnificent façade of Liberty, which is decked up for the holidays. You are drawn into the eternal embrace of the season by its tangible essence. When you enter, a world of elegance and beauty welcomes you. Christmastime in Liberty is a celebration of good taste and skilled workmanship. You are enticed to investigate the well-crafted displays that showcase a variety of carefully selected objects. Each decoration, designer trinkets as well as opulent textiles, is a work of art that has been specifically picked to capture the spirit of the season. The interior has a beautiful ambience that blends modernism and tradition. You are transported back in time by the wooden beams, famous wooden staircase, and elaborate embellishments. But despite its historical setting, there are modern designs and vogue-able styles that give the space a modern feel.

The welcoming staff, which is always eager to help and tell the origins of the works, adds to the atmosphere of warmth and delight. It's more than just a trip to the store; it's a journey through a tradition of style and grace. A joyful and welcoming atmosphere is created by the commotion of shopping and the soft hum of discussion.

- **Notting Hill:**

During the Christmas season, the lovely London neighborhood of Notting Hill dons a festive cloak. The festive energy of the season animates the charming buildings and cobblestone walkways. Everyone who enters this wonderful area of the city is welcomed by the air's expectancy and enthusiasm. There is something special about the shops in Notting Hill. Each one is a showcase for uniqueness and offers a variety of gems. You will discover a range of shopping hotspots, each with its personality, you will see cute boutiques and vintage shops. The spectacular decorations in the storefront windows urge onlookers to enter and investigate.

The thrill of finding unique presents at small stores cannot be overstated. You're sure to find something unique among the incredible variety of things, maybe you will become attracted to stylish clothing or even rare books. The merchants enhance the whole experience by being enthusiastic and affable while telling tales about their products. These beautiful shops are found in well-known Notting Hill areas including Notting Hill Road, Portobello Road, and Westbourne Grove. Each street's unique design and architecture add to the rustic allure of the neighborhood. The buildings' vivid hues contrast with the background of the holiday decorations to create a magnificent image that heightens the festive mood. Notting Hill is more than just a place to shop over the holidays. It's a celebration of both individualism and community. For those looking for a special and memorable Christmas experience in London, this area is a must-visit since the festive spirit of the season melds well with the creative essence of the area.

Finding unusual presents in London is an exploration full of thinking and discovery. Each gift stands for a bond, a sign of affection and gratitude for the receiver. You have a variety of alternatives for finding that ideal, unique present that will warm hearts and make lasting memories thanks to the artisan markets and boutique shops that dot the city.

Giving and volunteering over the holiday season in London: Spreading Joy

Christmas is about sharing, giving, and spreading pleasure rather than simply getting gifts. London has a variety of volunteer and charitable giving options during the Christmas season. It's a warm approach to improving people's lives and embracing the genuine spirit of the holiday season.

There are a ton of donation stations and collecting campaigns spread out over London, particularly around Christmas. These campaigns seek to gather necessities like warm clothes, blankets, canned goods, and toiletries. The goal is to help homeless people and families who are in need during the chilly winter months. People can easily donate to the cause thanks to the collecting locations put up by several charities, organizations, and neighborhood businesses. Food banks are essential in helping people in need get meals. Many people and families find it difficult to pay for meals during

Christmas. Non-perishable food donations can have a big influence on food banks. There are also volunteer possibilities in community centers and soup kitchens, which provide hot meals to the less fortunate. A satisfying approach to convey the joy of the holidays is to volunteer your time to serve meals. Christmas is a happy time for kids, but sadly not all kids get to enjoy the enchantment of the season. Toy drives are organized by several groups to collect toys for needy kids. Giving new, unopened items will make children happy and help them make special holiday memories.

People in London have a platform to give by giving gently used goods including clothes, books, furniture, and more to charity stores. The earnings from the sale of these goods are subsequently donated to charity organizations. These stores are valuable resources for volunteering, making donations, and supporting a variety of organizations. Making a difference in people's lives directly by volunteering is an effective strategy.

Many charities and shelters need volunteers over the Christmas season to help with a variety of duties, including serving meals, planning events, wrapping presents, and more. You can decide to personally participate in bringing happiness and gladness over the holiday season by getting your hands dirty. Throughout the Christmas season, London holds several charity events, campaigns, and fundraisers. These gatherings are planned to collect money for a variety of purposes, including healthcare and education. Participating in or making a donation to these events will assist in giving individuals in need much-needed assistance.

In addition to improving the lives of others, giving and volunteering during the London Christmas season allows you to appreciate the pleasure of giving. It's a chance for the community to get together and brighten the holiday season for everybody.

OFF THE BEATEN PATH ADVENTURES FOR CHRISTMAS IN LONDON

Hidden Gems & Secret Locations in London to Visit During Christmas

London has several secret locations and hidden jewels that spring to life during the Christmas season among the crowded streets and well-known tourist sites. Locals and tourists seeking an unusual but magical holiday experience like these spots.

❖ **The Columbia Road Flower Market:**

Located in London's East End, Columbia Road Flower Market is a bustling sanctuary that transforms beautifully throughout the holiday. This bustling market, which is generally recognized for its blooms, transforms into a festive extravaganza. The market dons a festive garment as winter wraps itself around the atmosphere. Normally filled with flowers, the booths are now filled with a symphony of wreaths, holly, and mistletoe. An amazing sensation is produced by the interaction of the colors and scents. A visual treat is going throughout the holiday season. It's interesting to see the chilly air contrasted with the celebratory flowers' warm tones. Each booth serves as an artist's palette and the market transforms into a vibrant painting, displaying a combination of seasonal greenery and conventional ornamentation.

The enthusiasm is contagious. The market is filled with excited shoppers who are shrouded in scarves and jackets. The sounds of conversation, laughing, and the clinking of purchases combine to provide a happy symphony that is a staple of the holiday atmosphere. The sellers provide a window into their world because they are enthusiastic about what they do. They tell how each wreath is painstakingly made and how each holly branch is carefully picked. It offers a look into the commitment and passion that go into making the holiday season lovely for other people. Christmastime at Columbia Road Flower Market is an immersion into the spirit of the holiday. It is a place where creativity, nature, and celebrations coexist together, leaving guests with a lasting recollection of the joyful celebration and the breathtaking natural beauty that adorns the center of London..

❖ **Little Venice:**

For those looking for a peaceful getaway over the Christmas season, London's Little Venice is a hidden treasure. During the holiday season, this small sanctuary, which is studded with picturesque rivers and beautiful canals located at Regent's park, comes alive with a unique attraction. Little Venice dons a colorful robe as winter extends a soft hug. The stillness of the river and the gorgeous surroundings are still there but are now emphasized by the reflections of glistening lights on the ripples. It provides a respite from the typical holiday bustle since it is a peaceful refuge within the busy metropolis. The decorated boats stand as floating displays of pleasure in this serene setting. Each boat tells a different tale and is decorated with lights and garlands that mimic the stars overhead. The scene is captivating and serves as a reminder of the season's understated but deep beauty. The freshness of the air as you stroll along the canals adds to the enchanted atmosphere. The gently sung holiday songs blend with the sounds of laughing and pleasure coming from surrounding homes as they resound through the canals. It is a soothing reminder of the unity that the season provides, a symphony of comfort and tranquility.

Little Venice during Christmas Time is a portal to another planet. It's an invitation to experience the beauty of the holiday season in a special environment while embracing the calm. It offers a revitalizing perspective on the festive mood in the center of London as it celebrates nature, calm, and shared moments of peace.

❖ Leadenhall Market

Leadenhall Market, a Victorian marvel in the heart of London, comes to life with a mystical air during the holiday season. Nestled in Gracechurch Street, its elaborate roof and cobblestone flooring provide a vibrant painting that combines custom with holiday celebrations. Winter brings about a modest change in the market. As the day becomes shorter and the wonderful lights come on, the magnificent building, which has been decked with wreaths and garlands, acquires a particular shine. It transforms into a sanctuary of holiday cheer, reflecting the happiness in the air.

The jovial decorations blend with a feeling of timeless beauty among the ancient arches. Normally a paradise for shopping, the booths are transformed into a beautiful visual feast. The vendors contribute to the festive ambiance by dressing up their items with holiday decorations, luring guests to explore this delightful corner. The joyful atmosphere is enhanced by the happy shoppers who are wrapped in warm scarves and caps. Their banter and laughing mingled with the music of the street performers to make a mesmerizing symphony. It looks like a scene out of a Christmas story, and the festive mood is in the air. Leadenhall Market is a celebration of solidarity and a trip through history. Under the canopy of this architectural wonder, people from all walks of life congregate to share happy memories and special moments.

Christmastime at Leadenhall Market is a lovely combination of tradition and celebration. It's a place where the past and present coexist and everyone is embraced by the Christmas spirit. It's a call to leave the commonplace behind and experience the remarkable wonder of the moment as you meander through a timeless setting.

❖ **God's Own Junkyard**

God's Own Junkyard, which is situated in Walthamstow, East London(Unit 12 Ravenswood Industrial Estate Shernhall Street), is a colorful tapestry of neon lights and unique patterns that change over the Christmas season. This fascinating place, which is a refuge for lovers of neon art, celebrates the holiday season with its special flare. The neon lights inside this creative treasure trove take on a vivid color when winter showers the city. The displays, which were previously animated, are now dancing to holiday music. The room is illuminated with cheery messages, bright reindeer, and vibrant ornaments, creating an electrifying kaleidoscope of light and color.

It seems like you're lost in a creative utopia as you make your way through the labyrinth of neon signs. The carefully designed lights, which come in a variety of forms and designs, exemplify the joy of the season. The buzz of electricity and the anticipation of seeing the stunning displays fill the air. God's Own Junkyard stands out at Christmas because of its unique philosophy. The neon lights, which are emblematic of urban style, take on a festive air and provide a distinctive and modern interpretation of the holiday mood. It provides a contemporary twist to the typical holiday atmosphere as a celebration of originality and uniqueness.

This creative retreat has an aura that can only be described as amazing. A sensory symphony is produced by the clash of colors, the commotion of tourists, and the buzzing of the neon lights. It's a place where the Christmas spirit is reinterpreted via a neon kaleidoscope, enabling guests to embrace the wonder of the season in an outlandish but alluring manner. Christmastime at God's Own Junkyard is proof that creativity, fantasy, and celebration can coexist. It's an invitation to enter a world of dazzling lights and creative energy, where the enchantment of the holidays is reinvented and celebrated in a unique and cutting-edge way..

❖ **Daunt Books**

Daunt Books, located at 83 Marylebone high street, creates a cozy and welcoming atmosphere over the holiday. With winter in the city and the holiday mood in full swing, this lovely bookstore's appeal has increased. Entering Daunt Books is like stepping into a world of literature. The year's favorite books are displayed on hardwood shelves that have subtle Christmas accents. The snug nooks are illuminated by the flickering glow of gentle lights, enticing book lovers to explore and get lost in the pages.

The aroma of freshly printed papers and freshly made coffee fills the air. The background music of traditional carols blends with the soothing sounds of pages flipping. In this setting, where the spirit of the season is woven into the very fabric of the room, visitors are transported to a world of literary joy. The personnel, who are renowned for their love of books and welcoming manner, give the event a personal touch. They eagerly participate in chats about their preferred authors and genres while also making suggestions. It's the ideal place for book lovers looking for the ideal book to curl up with on a cold night. Daunt Books is a haven for the enquiring mind and the weary spirit. It's a place where the literary and Christmas magic effortlessly converge. It serves as an invitation to enjoy reading, find comfort in the written word, and take in the magic of the holiday season in the center of London.

You will uncover a distinct aspect of the city's festive atmosphere by exploring these lesser explored treasures and secret locations during Christmas in London. Each location provides a unique and alluring experience, offering a lovely diversion from the more well-known sights.

Exploring London's Lesser-Known Wonders for Christmas: Offbeat Attractions

London is a city of hidden wonders, many of which are still unknown to the average tourist. Stepping off the main route over the holiday season opens up a world of unusual encounters and sights that reveal the city's lesser-known but no less charming nooks.

❖ **Wilton's Music Hall:**

Wilton's Music Hall is a historic landmark in 1 Graces Alley of the Eastern London neighborhood of Whitechapel. The oldest continuously operating music hall in the world, it adorns itself with a special charm during the holiday when the city is graced with its presence. Wilton's Music Hall changes into a wonderful world when the days get shorter and winter sets in. Christmas joy fills the historic hall, which is softly lighted and steeped in history. Elegant and subtle traditional decorations elegantly cover the old walls. During the holidays, entering this musical heaven is like entering a classic Christmas story. Visitors are taken back in time by the hazy aroma of aged wood and the soft seasonal music. A cozy, nostalgic atmosphere is created by the flickering illumination of old chandeliers. The pleasure of seeing a Christmas show here should be treasured. Each note and movement is given a unique enchantment by the skilled performers, the classic aesthetics, and the tangible feeling of history. It's a private event where the spectators share in a lovely, brief moment frozen in time.

Christmastime at Wilton's Music Hall attracts both history buffs and people looking for a distinctive holiday experience. Visitors will see the beauty of Christmas through the prism of history in this area where the past and present coexist together. It's an invitation to enjoy the holiday season while being embraced by bygone times and the echoes of the past.

❖ **Sir John Soane's Museum:**

The intriguing world of Sir John Soane's Museum is located in 13 Lincoln's Inn Fields, right in the middle of London. This architectural wonder, which was previously the residence of neo-classical architect Sir John Soane, acquires a special charm during the holidays. The museum plans a spectacular Christmas Evening event as winter covers the city. Under the warm glow of candlelight, the dimly lit chambers, each nook steeped in history, come to life. The exhibitions and relics get a timeless feel from the captivating shadows cast by the flickering flames.

The experience of seeing this museum during the holidays is similar to traveling back in time. The soft dance of candlelight enhances the antique furnishings, the classical sculptures, and the well-managed collections. It is a visceral encounter in which history whispers its stories and where jubilation and awe coexist. A traditional but exquisite holiday celebration is seen in part at the Christmas Evening event. The care taken to maintain and exhibit the architectural splendor enhances the charm of the season. It's a chance to savor the warmth of the holiday season while appreciating the workmanship of a bygone period. Christmastime at Sir John Soane's Museum is an opportunity to see history and art freshly. It's a voyage through time where the past and present delicately cross paths. It's a getaway from the hectic contemporary into a chic, magical environment where the true meaning of Christmas has been maintained for all time.

❖ **The Hunterian Museum**

The Hunterian Museum, located inside The Royal College of Surgeons 38-43 Lincoln's Inn Fields, is a fascinating collection. This one-of-a-kind museum, which is devoted to medical history, provides a special Christmastime experience. The museum cordially encourages visitors to browse its collection despite the chilly winter weather. The rooms are filled with fascinating species and relics, and they give off a serene wonder. A link between science and history is created by the well-kept displays that illustrate how surgery and medical knowledge have developed through time. The Hunterian Museum offers a strange yet intriguing juxtaposition throughout the holiday season. The exhibition's scientific focus contrasts with Christmas' festive atmosphere. It's a chance to consider development, learning, and human growth while enjoying the happiness and cohesion that characterize the Christmas season.

Visitors' murmurs as they pass from display to show create a polite but enquiring symphony. The relics appear to come to life with tales of discovery and tenacity, reminding us that the spirit of inquiry is ageless, even in the field of science. Christmas at the Hunterian Museum provides more than simply a look into the past of medicine. It is a study of human creativity and a tribute to curiosity and education. For individuals who want to comprehend both the scientific and joyful parts of life, it is a place where the wonder of discovery blends with the magic of the holiday season.

Visiting these unusual sights at Christmas in London is a chance to go off the beaten path. Each location provides a unique and engaging experience that enables travelers to explore the less well-known but no less enchanting areas of the city. It's an opportunity to embrace the unexpected and make lasting memories apart from the usual holiday routine.

Exploring Creativity in London's Independent Boutiques and Art Galleries

During the Christmas season, London, a city brimming with creativity, turns into a paradise of artistry and ingenuity. In the middle of the holiday happiness, independent shops and art galleries beckon, enticing residents and tourists to explore one-of-a-kind and creative masterpieces.

❖ **Tate Modern Shop**

The Tate Modern Shop, located on 53 Bankside, the center of London's creative district, emerges as a treasure trove for art lovers, particularly during Christmas. The museum, a massive icon of modern art, is home to a store that supports its mission. The Tate Modern Shop transforms when winter enfolds the city. The area has a festive atmosphere, and visitors are drawn in by the windows' beautiful displays. All are warmly welcomed to a world where giving and art coexist at the entrance, which is surrounded by colorful banners. When one enters, a variety of creative works welcome them. The shelves are stacked with prints, postcards, and books, each of which tells a tale of contemporary art. The air is filled with the soft buzz of other art lovers, a subliminal reminder that creation is a shared passion. For those looking for a piece of art to keep or give as a present, the store is a haven. It provides a variety of options, like elaborate jewelry inspired by well-known pieces and exquisite stationery embellished with creative themes. Every visitor will find something they like thanks to the well-chosen range that caters to a variety of preferences.

The Tate Modern Shop's appeal comes from its capacity to provide more than simply goods; it offers an aesthetic experience. The items, which are a continuation of the museum's collection, arouse feelings and stimulate the mind. It serves as a conduit for transferring a work of contemporary art's soul outside of gallery spaces. This creative paradise becomes a center for gift-giving inventiveness around Christmas. Every object appears to vibrate with the holiday happiness as the holiday spirit blends with the creative mood. It's a place to find presents that showcase creativity, a manifestation of the cheerful season, and an invitation to everyone to share a passion for art during the most delightful season of the year.

❖ **House of Illustration**

The House of Illustration is tucked away in King's Cross at 2 Granary Square, a bustling area of London. As winter adorns the city and the holiday season approaches, this wonderful creative space; a home for artists and enthusiasts; takes on a unique attraction. During the holiday season, entering the House of Illustration will be like entering a vibrant, alive world of art. The excitement that hangs in the air is mixed with the smell of paper and ink. The well-lit spaces are alive with a sense of celebration and creativity, and they are decorated with appealing artwork. The hallways, which include a variety of displays, beckon investigation. Each movement of the artist's pen or brush conveys a narrative, evoking emotions and revealing imagination. The artwork of the artists, which is presented on walls and in books, invites the viewer to explore their creative process. The gift store, where creative marvels are translated into delightful goods, is the center of this artistic domicile. The store is a gold mine for people looking for creative treasures to present and keep, with everything; treasures like prints that capture the spirit of artwork as well as postcards that communicate stories via photographs.

The House of Illustration is a combination of creativity and celebration. It's a place where the enchantment of the holidays and the wonder of creation are entwined. It embraces creativity and the beauty of expression, serving as a reminder to all who enter that art permeates all aspects of life, not only what is shown on the walls.

❖ **The Mosaic Rooms**

The Mosaic Rooms located right in the middle of Kensington at Tower House 226 Cromwell Road. This cultural sanctuary has a special appeal throughout the holiday season when winter covers the city. Visitors are welcomed into a world of art and culture by the entryway, which is decorated in a modest but magnificent manner. The interior's dark lighting gives a sense of mystery and encourages exploration. The many displays housed in each area make the spaces come to life with imagination.

A festive vibe permeates the space among the well-collected paintings. The fusion of creative exhibits and the festive atmosphere produces a unique experience where the enjoyment of the season and art appreciation come together. The gift store, a continuation of this creative home, has a wide variety of gifts. It is a haven for individuals looking for unique presents that connect with the spirit of creation, handmade jewelry and art-inspired souvenirs. The Mosaic Rooms represent cultural festivity more than any other place throughout the Christmas season. It's an opportunity to embrace the holiday spirit while investigating various creative genres. It serves as a reminder that both the Christmas season and art benefit lives by fostering creativity and the beauty of expression.

❖ The Fan Museum

The Fan Museum is located at 12 Crooms Hill, amid the wintry allure of London. This museum, an elegant refuge devoted to the art of fans, takes on a unique appeal throughout the holiday season. The museum's facade warmly greets guests with a subdued show of holiday cheer as it is tucked away in the historic center of Greenwich. A realm of subtle beauty unfolds as one enters. The elaborate fans, which are like little works of art, come to life in the soft light of the strategically positioned lights. There is a faint aroma of workmanship and nostalgia in the air. A sensation of time travel is evoked by the passageways, which are decorated with fans from different decades. Each carefully constructed fan offers a story of creative mastery and bygone grandeur. The museum's amazing gift store has a wide selection of items made with fan inspiration. It's a haven for individuals looking for one-of-a-kind, artistic gifts that embody the spirit of the season, tiny trinkets and complex hand fans. The Fan Museum celebrates creativity and refinement throughout the holiday season rather than just being a monument to fan-making. It's a call to respect the past and enjoy the delicate. It serves as a reminder that even in the middle of the celebrations, beauty endures and art continues to dazzle all who enter.

Christmastime exploration of these small shops and art galleries is an invitation to explore London's vibrant creative scene. It's a chance to celebrate the beauty of creativity and creative expression while appreciating the many genres of artistic expression and finding remarkable, meaningful presents that capture the essence of the holiday season.

WALKING TOURS WITH A TWIST

Alternative Walking Tours: A Christmas Look at London's Quirky Side

During the holiday season, a fresh experience awaits in London's busy streets: a trip through the city's most eccentric neighborhoods. Those looking for a unique holiday experience are drawn to these eccentric pursuits.

❖ **Street Art Tour - The Colors of Yuletide Expression**

Explore the colorful street art scene that graces London's nooks and crannies. The metropolitan landscape changes during the holiday season, its colors expressing tales of the occasion. Brick walls transform into festive pages as you go by, exhibiting ingenuity in the most unlikely settings.

- **Shoreditch**

Explore the lively, outdoor art gallery that is Shoreditch. The East End of London, is where Shoreditch is situated. Within the London Borough of Hackney, it is renowned for its artistic and creative culture, vivid street art, cutting-edge fashion scene, and diverse nightlife. For those looking for a distinctive and exciting neighborhood experience in London, Shoreditch has grown to be a favorite destination among foodies, art lovers, and others. Christmastime sees the walls come alive with creative depictions of the season.

- **Brick Lane**

Stroll along Brick Lane to see murals that perfectly express the joy of the season. It is situated in the Tower Hamlets neighborhood of London's East End. It's a well-known street that's noted for its bright street art, rich ethnic variety, and lively scene of markets, stores, cafés, and curry places. In addition to housing a bustling creative population, Brick Lane has established itself as a famous destination for art, fashion, and gastronomy. It is a vibrant painting that captures the wonder and excitement of Christmas.

- **Leake Street Tunnel**

Explore this graffiti hotspot, which is always changing. The Leake Street Tunnel, commonly referred to as the "Banksy Tunnel," is situated under the platforms of Waterloo station in the Waterloo district of London. It is a well-known location for street art and graffiti, where creators are free to legally produce and exhibit their works. The tunnel has developed into a dynamic gallery that draws people and artists from all over the globe to see London's vibrant street art culture. The tunnel exhibits a variety of artistic expression, including original works of Christmas-themed art.

- **Camden**

Experience Camden's unique appeal, where festive happiness and street art coexist. A neighborhood in London's northwest. The region, which is a part of the London Borough of Camden, is well-known for its lively markets, eccentric shops, a variety of music venues, and an alternative cultural scene. With its variety of entertainment, street art, culinary choices, and unusual combination of subcultures, Camden is a well-liked destination for both visitors and residents. A creative adventure with a hint of holiday enchantment will be found on the streets.

- **East End Streets**

Explore the East End's streets and the murals that grace the buildings there, which use an urban aesthetic vocabulary to convey stories of Christmas. A region in the eastern portion of downtown London, that encompasses several East End enclaves and thoroughfares, including Shoreditch, Brick Lane, Whitechapel, and Spitalfields. This region is renowned for its rich history, street art, marketplaces, and vibrant artistic and creative community. Located in the eastern portion of the city, East End Streets is a center of innovation and offers a distinctive fusion of contemporary trends and historical relevance.

❖ **Yuletide Tales in Hidden Libraries**

There is a charming adventure via secret libraries and literary hotspots for book enthusiasts. Consider reading Christmas stories in quaint book nooks. It is a literary voyage, a celebration of storytelling, and a special way to get into the Christmas season.

• **The British Library**

Visit The British Library to explore its stunning collections and changing exhibitions. Located at 96 Euston Road. It is conveniently accessible from downtown London due to its location close to King's Cross and St. Pancras International train stations. One of the biggest and most well-known libraries in the world, the British Library is recognized for its vast collection of books, manuscripts, and other materials. Find stories about

Christmases from many ages and civilizations scattered throughout the books.

- **The London Library**

Explore the depths of The London Library, where both classic and modern literature, resonating with the spirit of the season, bring the enchantment of Christmas to life. It is conveniently located at 14 St. James Square among other well-known attractions and cultural organizations in the city and is located in the center of London. A notable private lending library, The London Library is renowned for its huge book collection and its historical significance in the literary world.

- **The Wiener Collection**

Take a look at the inspiring tales of resiliency and hope at The Wiener Library, which is devoted to the study of the Holocaust. It is located in the Bloomsbury neighborhood of downtown London, at 29 Russell Square. A vast collection of records, publications, and archives about the Holocaust and other genocides are kept in the Wiener Library, a famous institution devoted to genocide studies and Holocaust history. During the Christmas season, it serves as a space for understanding and contemplation.

- **Maughan Library**

Visit King's College London's historical jewel, The Maughan Library. It is close to Chancery Lane in downtown London. King's College London's Maughan Library is renowned for its stunning architecture and substantial collection of scholarly materials. Read classic Christmas stories among the opulence and take in the holiday spirit inside the walls of this hidden gem.

- **Wellcome Collection**

Enjoy The Wellcome Collection Reading Room to its fullest. It is conveniently located in the heart of London at 183 Euston Road, and is adjacent to other renowned institutions. The Wellcome Collection is well-known for its exhibits and holdings that unite science, health, life, and art to provide visitors a richer experience. Engage in literary works that explore the wonders of human existence to create a special Christmas reading experience.

- **Marx Memorial Library**

Explore The Marx Memorial Library's intellectual universe. It is located at 37A Clerkenwell Green, which is renowned for its historical and cultural value, on Clerkenwell Green. For information and study on Marxism, socialism, and the lives and works of Karl Marx and Friedrich Engels, turn to the Marx Memorial Library. Discover historical viewpoints and tales about Christmas and the holiday spirit as you peruse its shelves.

Through the pages of books, these secret libraries provide a look into the magic of Christmas. They provide a tranquil haven where the warmth of Yuletide stories can be experienced, where the enchantment of storytelling meets the magic of the season.

❖ **London's   Underground   Secrets: Underground History Tour**

A maze of historical secrets is hidden underneath the city's busy streets. Explore secret passages and abandoned rooms as you set out on a subterranean adventure. It's a historical voyage that unearths stories of long-forgotten Christmases that are just waiting to be discovered.

● **Churchill War Rooms**

The Churchill War Rooms invites you to descend into the depths of history. Find out where Winston Churchill and his administration managed operations during World War II in these subterranean bunkers. The Churchill War Rooms are located in the center of Westminster, next to St. James's Park and the Houses of Parliament at King Charles Street, Clive Steps. Visitors can tour the subterranean bunkers where Winston Churchill and his administration oversaw activities during World War II at this famous historical location. Experience the ambiance of battle while learning about the important events that occurred during Christmas.

- **Clapham South Subterranean Shelter Tour**

Discover the Clapham South Deep-Level Shelter's secret location. It is deeply below and was built during World War II as an air raid bunker. It is situated in Clapham at Balham Hill, a neighborhood in southern London. A historic subterranean location, the Clapham South deep-level bunker was first built as an air raid shelter during World War II to shield residents from bombardment. Today, it provides a distinctive window into the city's history and the part it played in trying times. You will discover its history and the part it played during the wartime Christmas season throughout your trip.

- **The Postal Museum's Mail Rail**

The Postal Museum offers tours of London's subterranean postal system. The Postal Museum, located in the center of London at 15-20 Phoenix

Place, presents the development of the postal system. This museum's postal Rail, which takes you on an underground tour into the mysterious world of London's legendary postal delivery system, is a fascinating feature. It provides a unique viewpoint on how mail was delivered underneath the city's streets, making it an interesting and instructive experience. You will experience for yourself a hidden world underneath the city on the Mail Rail journey, which emphasizes the value of communication.

- **The Thames Tunnel and the Brunel Museum**

At the Brunel Museum, learn about the mysteries of the Thames Tunnel. This ancient tunnel was an engineering wonder that offered a unique experience at the time. The Brunel Museum, which is close to the River Thames at the Brunel Engine House Railway Avenue, sheds light on the extraordinary engineering of the Thames Tunnel. One of the world's first underwater tunnels, the tunnel is a historical wonder. You will learn more about this museum's creation and influence on the advancement of transportation by touring it. It's an interesting voyage through London's technical achievements in the past. Discover its depths and find out more about London's past, including what it will be like around Christmas.

You will go back in time and picture the city's past during the joyous Christmas season by visiting these locations, which provide an intriguing look into London's secret subterranean history.

❖ **Green Spaces Tour - A Seasonal Walk Through Nature's Art**

Take a tour of London's green havens to get away from the city's hustle and bustle. A tranquil stroll through parks and gardens decorated with seasonal greenery is encouraged. In the middle of the holiday hustle, nature serves as the artist, creating a picture of Christmas on a canvas using a palette of greens and browns.

- **Kew Gardens**

Take a tour of this floral paradise. The gardens still exude seasonal beauty in the winter, reflecting the brilliance of nature via breathtaking displays and joyful energy. It's a little southwest of the city's core in the London neighborhood of Richmond. A huge botanical park, Kew Gardens is renowned for its wide variety of plants, trees, and stunning scenery. Particularly during the Christmas season, when it often has unique seasonal decorations, it's a sweet and calm spot for a stroll, to learn about plants, and to take in the beauty of nature.

- **Regent's Park**

Explore this opulent park by taking a walk in it. Discover the park's natural craftsmanship as it is decorated for Christmas with sparkling lights and a festive mood. It is located in central London's northwest, close to the Marylebone and Fitzrovia neighborhoods at Chester Road. Regent's Park is a magnificent green area renowned for its well-maintained gardens, open areas, and a lovely lake. It's a wonderful location for strolls, picnics, and outdoor enjoyment, particularly during the holiday season when it could feature festive decorations and activities.

- **Richmond Green**

where nature's artistic creations are on full show. The park provides a peaceful haven at Christmas with its festive appeal and the elegance of animals. It is well situated in 300 upper Richmond, a lovely neighborhood southwest of Central London. Richmond Green is a beautiful open area surrounded by trees and old structures. People visit this area to relax, play games, have picnics, and enjoy the foliage, particularly around Christmas when it has this festive feel to enhance its already stunning natural beauty.

- **Hampstead Heath**

Explore the trails of London's Hampstead Heath, a piece of nature's art. Witness the splendor of the heath decorated with a hint of Christmas, fusing the joy of the season with the majesty of nature. It is situated in the Hampstead lane neighborhood in central London's northwest. The huge, lovely Hampstead Heath is famed for its hills, ponds, and breathtaking vistas of the city. People come here to go on walks, fly kites, or just take in the scenery. It's a tranquil retreat during Christmastime, providing an opportunity to take in the splendor of nature in a joyful setting.

- **Victoria Park**

Enjoy a stroll through this gorgeous green environment. The park is decked up with colorful lights and ornaments throughout the Christmas season, bringing a little bit of enchantment to nature's canvas. It is located in London's East End, close to the communities of Bethnal Green and Hackney at old ford road. Victoria Park is a popular park that provides a range of outdoor sports, peaceful walks, and stunning lake views. Christmastime festivities in this picturesque area of London can include special activities or decorations in the park.

- **Battersea Park**

Take a leisurely walk around Battersea Park, where the surrounding natural beauty is enhanced by seasonal decorations and festive lighting, creating a beautiful environment. London. At central London's southwest neighborhood, close to the River Thames and the well-known Battersea Power Station. A lovely park featuring gardens, a lake, and sports facilities. People often go there for outdoor activities like picnics, strolls, or just to relax. With holiday decorations and festivities, it may have a wonderful, joyous mood throughout Christmas.

- **Greenwich Park**

Enjoy the festive splendor of nature by taking a stroll in Greenwich Park. The park provides serene surroundings and breathtaking vistas throughout the holiday season. Southeast of London's downtown is the Greenwich neighborhood where it is located. The breathtaking vistas of the River Thames, the Prime Meridian Line, and the Royal Observatory can all be found at Greenwich Park, a historic royal park. Visitors can take advantage of the walking trails, stunning scenery, and tranquil respite from the city. The park has this festive feel around Christmas, making it even more enjoyable for visitors.

- **Brockwell Park**

During the holidays, explore Brockwell Park's delights. The park's scenery changes with the spirit of Christmas, making for a pleasant stroll into the wilderness. It is situated close to the communities of Brixton and Herne Hill in the southern region of central London at 117 Norwood Road. A wonderful park, Brockwell Park has large open spaces, a lido, and exquisite plants. People go there to unwind, go on picnics, and engage in different outdoor pursuits.

It's a calm area during Christmas Time where you may stroll and take in the festive ambiance.

- **Wimbledon and Putney Commons**

Discover Wimbledon Common's artistic nature over the holiday season. In the thick of the holiday season, the expansive greenery and serene pathways provide a welcome getaway. They are situated close to Wimbledon and Putney in the southwest region of London. Large protected green spaces like these commons are great for taking a refreshing stroll, having a picnic, or just relaxing in nature. The commons provide a tranquil haven throughout the holiday season, enabling guests to take in the natural splendor.

- **Crystal Palace Park**

Take pleasure in a holiday stroll in Crystal Palace Park, where the cheery holiday atmosphere enhances the beauty of nature. The arrangement of the park and the tranquil waters provide a beautiful scene. It is close to the Crystal Palace district in the south of London at Thicket Road. The park is renowned for its historical connections and distinctive characteristics, which include the ruins of the Crystal Palace, lakes, and greenery. Visitors come for strolls, picnics, and to take in the picturesque surroundings. The park takes on a distinct charm during Christmas, making it a beautiful place to celebrate the season.

- **Holland Park**

Explore Holland Park, which is renowned for its opulent gardens and breathtaking views. The park is decorated with lights around Christmas, which heightens the attractiveness of its uncultivated beauty. It is situated close to Notting Hill and Kensington in central London's western region. Holland Park is a lovely park that is well-known for its stately gardens, tranquil atmosphere, and the old Holland House. People often go to the park to unwind, stroll, or just take in the peace. It's a beautiful location to enjoy a mix of nature and a dash of holiday enchantment throughout the holiday season.

With the beauty of the outdoors and the enchantment of Christmas, these extra green places provide a perfect chance to immerse yourself in the seasonal charm of nature.

These non-traditional walking excursions provide a unique perspective on London's holiday mood. They are a call to embrace the unexpected, deviate from the beaten route, and uncover the city's more eccentric and endearing side during the enchanted Christmas season.

Thames Riverside Walks: Beautiful Christmas Walks

It is a lovely experience to tour the Thames Riverside Walks during the holiday season in London. A beautiful atmosphere is produced by the crisp air, the warm glow of the streetlights, and the picturesque vistas of the river. You can decide to take these beautiful strolls along the Thames at the following locations:

- **The South Bank**

A traditional option is to stroll along the South Bank of the Thames. The London Eye's dazzling lights, the commotion of street performers, and the river's steady flow make it the ideal location for a holiday promenade. It is situated on the southern bank of the River Thames, just across from the city's center. The picturesque riverbank walks, thriving cultural scene, and well-known attractions like the London Eye are all highlights of this region. You will enjoy a variety of activities while strolling along the South Bank, visiting art galleries as well as taking in performances by street performers. You also get a lovely perspective of the city skyline. It's a great location to experience the excitement of the city and the allure of the Thames River.

- **London Bridge to Tower Bridge**

Start close to the well-known Tower Bridge and go toward London Bridge. This section provides breathtaking views of the Thames, and the reflection of the bridge lights in the water creates a festive and tranquil ambiance. It is a section of the River Thames, which flows through the heart of London. Starting from London Bridge, you should take a beautiful stroll down the Thames while admiring the sights of both ancient and contemporary sites. You'll drive by famous landmarks including the Shard and the Tower of London before arriving at the charming Tower Bridge. This path is a lovely promenade for both inhabitants and tourists to the city since it combines history, beautiful architecture, and the majesty of the Thames.

- **Richmond to Twickenham**

Give yourself a thrill from Twickenham to Richmond For a pleasant stroll. You will savor the tranquil beauty of the Thames by strolling along the riverbank route, which has a blend of natural and man-made structures.

- **Hammersmith to Chiswick**

Start from Hammersmith Bridge and stroll in the direction of Chiswick. This walk offers a tranquil but interesting Christmas stroll by blending greenery and urban views.

- **Vauxhall to Westminster**

Make your way to Vauxhall Bridge starting from the area of Westminster Bridge. This stroll is made very enthralling by the vistas of Parliament, the London Eye, and the city lights reflected off the Thames.

- **Thames Barrier Park**

Discover the contemporary, creative twist of the Thames Barrier Park. The calm of the river combined with the park's design makes for a unique vacation experience. It is located close to the River Thames in the eastern section of London at North Woolwich Road. Due to its cutting-edge architecture and intended function as a barrier against high tides, this park is distinctive. It's a wonderful place to go for a calm stroll, to take in the scenery, and to breathe in the fresh air. A riverbank path, open areas, and rich plants are all present in the park. Away from the bustle of the city, it is a warm and pleasant spot to unwind.

These Thames Riverside Walks provide a superb chance to get into the holiday mood while admiring the river and its environs during the Christmas season in London.

ACCOMMODATIONS DURING CHRISTMAS IN LONDON

Bed and Breakfast: A Personalized Experience

- **Pooters Bed & Breakfast**

Pooters Bed & Breakfast, which is situated in a charming area of London at 23-24 Montague Street, becomes a joyful retreat during the holiday season. The rooms are decorated with happy décor, creating a warm and welcoming atmosphere. The atmosphere is lively, which makes your stay joyful and cheery. The price range for a nice vacation stay varies depending on the room choice and the exact dates, but it is cheap. For regular accommodation, rates normally range from £80 to £120 per night, depending on the style of room and availability. The best course of action is to always confirm the most up-to-date and accurate price with the B&B immediately.

- **Wimbledon Bed & Breakfast**

Wimbledon Bed & Breakfast provides a wonderful Christmas experience and is located in a peaceful area of London precisely at 131 Queens Road. The interior is warm and inviting, and the rooms are decked up for the holidays. A happy stay is guaranteed by the atmosphere's permeation with the festive spirit. Depending on the style of accommodation and availability, a normal room at Wimbledon Bed & Breakfast generally costs between £70 and £110 per night during the holiday season for a relaxing holiday getaway.

- **Fox Hill Bed & Breakfast**

The tranquil London bed and breakfast Fox Hill transforms into a holiday sanctuary during Christmas. The environment is welcoming and friendly, and it is decorated for the holidays. The air is filled with the festive atmosphere of the season, indicating a happy stay. The cost of regular accommodation over the Christmas season normally ranges from £90 to £130 per night, depending on the style of room and the precise dates. It is advised that you get in touch with the B&B directly to get the most precise and recent price information.

- **St John Bed & Breakfast**

During the holiday season, St John Bed & Breakfast in a tranquil area of London at 20 St. John's Way, provides a welcoming haven. The festive decorations add to the cozy and welcoming atmosphere. The holiday spirit is pervasive and assures a happy stay. A regular accommodation normally costs between £85 and £120 per night during the holiday season. But costs could change depending on the kind of accommodation and the precise dates.

- **Owlets Bed and Breakfast**

During the holiday season, Owlets Bed & Breakfast in a peaceful area of London (112 Arundel Avenue) provides a welcoming refuge. With lovely Christmas decorations, the ambiance is warm and welcoming. The atmosphere is festive, making for a happy and relaxing stay. A regular accommodation will normally cost between £75 and £110 per night during the holiday season. However, costs might change based on the choice of accommodation and particular dates.

- **Bay Tree House Bed & Breakfast**

The tranquil London neighborhood of Bay Tree House Bed & Breakfast situated at 59 Brookdale, is a great spot to spend the holiday season. Warm and inviting, the setting is embellished with holiday accents to create a festive mood. The Christmas mood is strong, which makes your stay joyful and enjoyable. A regular accommodation normally costs between £85 and £120 per night during the holiday season. But, costs might vary depending on the kind of accommodation and the precise dates.

Hostels and Guesthouses: Affordable Options for a Merry Stay

- **72qt Guest House**

The calm neighborhood of London's 72qt Guest House is a welcoming place to spend the holiday season situated at 72 Queensborough Terrace. The ambiance is cozy and welcoming, and the festive touches add to the happy mood. Christmas spirit is palpable, offering a joyful and joyful stay. Regular accommodation normally costs between £90 and £130 per night during the holiday season.

- **Hampstead Village Guesthouse**

During the Christmas season, Hampstead Village Guesthouse, which is situated in a picturesque area of London at 2 Kemplay Road, provides a warm getaway. The atmosphere is warm and welcoming, decorated for the holidays. There is a strong sense of the Christmas spirit, which makes for a happy and relaxing visit. A regular accommodation will normally cost between £95 and £140 per night during the holiday season.

- **The Lavender Guest House**

Located in a tranquil area of London (18 Lavender Sweep). The Lavender Guest House offers a warm retreat throughout the holiday season. The festive decorations add to the cozy and friendly environment. The holiday spirit is in the air, indicating a happy and relaxing stay. A regular accommodation normally costs between £80 and £120 per night during the Christmas season.

- **Wombat's The City Hostel London**

A lively place to spend the holiday season, which is situated in a bustling area of the city at Flat 7 17 Dock Street. The mood is festive and upbeat, with a feeling of community. The holiday atmosphere is contagious and ensures a joyful and joyful stay. A shared dormitory bed normally costs between £30 and £60 per night during the holiday season.

- **YHA London Oxford Street**

Located in a busy part of the city at 14 Noel Street, YHA London Oxford Street is a fun spot to stay throughout the holiday season. The atmosphere is vibrant and animated, evoking the festive mood. The contagious holiday spirit ensures a fun and lively visit. A shared dormitory bed might costs between £25 and £70 per night during the Christmas season.

- **The Dictionary Hostel**

The Dictionary Hostel London is a lively spot to spend the holiday season and is situated at 10-20 Kingsland Road. The joyful holiday mood is reflected in the lively and welcoming environment. There is a palpable sense of Christmas spirit, which forebodes a jovial and joyful stay. A regular accommodation costs between £40 and £120 per night during the Christmas season.

- **Park Villa Boutique Hostel**

In a picturesque area of London at 51 Grove Road, Park Villa Boutique Hostel provides a warm haven throughout the holiday. The festive mood is reflected in the atmosphere, which is warm and pleasant. The atmosphere is festive, guaranteeing a happy and comfortable stay. A shared dormitory bed costs between £35 and £90 per night during Christmas.

- **Palmers Lodge Swiss Cottage**

During the Christmas season, Palmers Lodge Swiss Cottage, located in a tranquil area of London, is a warm refuge. The setting is warm and welcoming, decorated for the holidays. There is a strong Christmas vibe, which suggests a happy and relaxing stay. A shared dormitory bed normally costs between £30 and £80 per night during the Christmas season. But costs could change depending on the kind of accommodation and the precise dates. It is advised to speak with the lodge directly for the most precise and recent pricing.

- **Safestay London Elephant & Castle**

Located at 144-152 Walworth Road, Safestay London Elephant & Castle is a fun spot to stay over the holiday season. The lively, upbeat environment reflects the joyous holiday spirit. There is a strong Christmas vibe, which suggests a happy and exciting stay. A shared dormitory bed normally costs between £25 and £70 per night during the holiday season.

Holiday Rentals and Apartments: Home Away from Home

- **Bankside Apartment at Borough Market #1**

In a busy area of London, Bankside Apartment at Borough Market #1 is a comfortable place to spend the holiday. The cheerful and energetic ambiance reflects the Christmas mood. The holiday spirit is palpable and promises a relaxing and happy stay. Typically, regular accommodation costs between £120 and £200 per night during the Christmas season.

- **Central Zone 1 Spacious Garden Apartment**

A great option to stay over the Christmas season is the Central Zone 1 Spacious Garden Apartment, which is situated in a desirable district of London. The setting is warm and welcoming, ideal for the Christmas season. The holiday spirit is in the air, making for a relaxing and enjoyable visit. During

Christmas, the cost of the full apartment normally varies from £150 to £300 each night.

- **Let's holiday in London Greenwich B1**

This is a nice place to celebrate the Christmas season and is tucked away in a bustling area of the city. It has a cozy, friendly atmosphere that is ideal for Christmas. The atmosphere is festive and joyful, making for a comfortable and delightful stay. During Christmas, the cost of the full apartment ranges from £90 to £180 each night.

- **Luxury Highly Functional Notting Hill Flat, Ideal for Singles and Couples**

In a hip part of London, the Luxury Highly Functional Notting Hill Flat is a terrific spot for singles or couples to stay during the holidays. The environment is chic and functional, making it ideal for a festive atmosphere. A pleasant and relaxing stay is guaranteed by the Christmas celebrations, which add to the charm. It normally costs between £180 to £300 per night for the full apartment over the Christmas season.

- **Spacious Apartment In Bloomsbury**

The Spacious Apartment in Bloomsbury is a great place to spend the holiday season since it's located in a bustling area of London at walking Distance To City & West End. Sleep 5. The atmosphere is open and inviting, perfect for getting into the festive mood. There is a festive atmosphere throughout, guaranteeing a fun and relaxed visit. During Christmas, the cost of the full apartment ranges from £120 to £250 each night.

Kid-Friendly Hotels: Entertainment and Comfort for the Little Ones

- **The Athenaeum Hotel & Residences**

Mayfair. For the joyous Christmas season, the Athenaeum Hotel & Residences in London is a fantastic option. It is situated in Mayfair, a prestigious area of the city, at 116 Piccadilly. Families will like the setting, which places a particular emphasis on giving children a memorable experience. The hotel goes all out for Christmas with seasonal accents and a pleasant atmosphere for everyone. In terms of price, a Christmas night's stay costs between £350 and £700, depending on the hotel style and facilities.

- **The Montague on The Gardens**

For a festive Christmas season getaway in London, choose The Montague on The Gardens. It is tucked away at 15 Montague Street in Bloomsbury and provides families with a warm and welcoming environment. The hotel is well recognized for producing a warm and joyous atmosphere during Christmas, making it a fantastic place to spend a special vacation. In terms of cost, a Christmas night's stay ranges from £280 to £500, depending on the facilities and room type.

- **The Rubens at the Palace**

For the joyous Christmas season, The Rubens at the Palace in London is a sweet option. The location, 39 Buckingham Palace Road, in Victoria, is ideal for holiday celebrations. The hotel is a wonderful place for a festive family stay since it extends a warm welcome to families and provides a pleasant Christmas experience with special packages and activities for kids. Price-wise, a Christmas night's stay should costs between £300 and £600, depending on the kind of accommodation and extras offered.

- **The Landmark London**

The Landmark London. It's conveniently located at 222 Marylebone Road and also a good place to spend the holidays. Especially for families wishing to spend the season, the hotel offers a cozy and joyous environment throughout Christmas, with unique activities and decorations that make the stay absolutely wonderful. In terms of cost, a Christmas night's stay normally ranges from £400 to £800.

TIPS FOR A MEMORABLE LONDON CHRISTMAS

Staying warm and fashionable while dressing for the weather

Christmastime in London is characterized by frigid, often rainy weather. The city has a moderate marine climate, which means that although it seldom gets particularly cold, it may be fairly windy and wet at times, making it seem colder than it really is.

Temperatures in December typically vary from 36 to 46 degrees Fahrenheit or 2 to 8 degrees Celsius. To resist the cold, it is essential to layer your clothing. A base layer made of thermal or moisture-wicking material should be the first layer, followed by a warm sweater or fleece, and finally a waterproof and windproof outer layer. To keep your extremities warm, don't forget a decent winter coat, gloves, a scarf, and a cap. Shoes are also very important. If you want to walk about the city or visit outdoor attractions, choose insulated, waterproof boots to keep your feet warm and dry. The socks must be warm. Think about the things you'll be doing while choosing your attire. Warmth and comfort should be given top priority if you want to spend a lot of time outside. However, London is a trendy city, so you can still have a chic appearance by dressing in warm layers and winter accessories.

Before leaving, check the weather forecast to assist you choose the appropriate attire for the day. Have an umbrella or a waterproof coat on hand to be ready for any potential downpour. You can enjoy your vacation, look well, and be comfortable by dressing for the weather in London during the Christmas season.

City Navigation: Travel and Transportation Tips

With a few travel tips and knowledge of the city's transit alternatives, navigating London over the holidays should be fun and feasible.

- The London Underground (Tube) is among the most practical modes of transportation in the city. It is a system of trains that will rapidly transport you across the city. Plan your visits carefully as it will be busier than normal over Christmas owing to the holiday rush. For a more affordable option to pay for your travel, look for an Oyster card.

- London has a robust bus system. Buses are a fantastic way to explore the city and its holiday lights. Trams are a different means of transportation that are present in various places.

- London has an abundance of taxis and ride-sharing services. They are a practical option, particularly if you're traveling in a group or have a lot of shopping to do. Just keep in mind that around the holidays, traffic will be worse.

- If you want to ride a bike, you can do it in London. There are designated bike lanes in several places. Just be sure to use protective gear and dress warmly.

- The River Thames flows through London, and river boat services are available to help you get about the city. Especially during the holidays, this will be a picturesque and distinctive mode of transportation.

- London is a city that encourages pedestrians. Walking is also a great way to take in the holiday spirit, particularly in neighborhoods with gorgeous Christmas lights like Oxford Street.

- Download travel applications to assist with route planning and to check for up-to-the-minute transit information. Google Maps is a well-liked option.

- To escape the crowds, think about going during off-peak times. It might be calmer in the mornings and early afternoons.

- Have a direction in mind and plan your routes before you go. This will help you save time and have a more enjoyable trip.

- Don't be afraid to approach station employees or locals for assistance if you need help with instructions or transit alternatives. The majority of folks are helpful and nice.

You will conveniently tour the lovely city of London during the joyous Christmas season by making use of these travel tips and taking into account the numerous transit alternatives.

Tips for a Happy Holiday: Staying Safe and Healthy

A happy experience during your London Christmas vacation depends on you feeling safe and secure. To ensure you have a fun and safe day, consider the following simple advice:

- Keep current with the most recent COVID-19 procedures and recommendations published by the government and health organizations. Observe social distancing practices, put on masks when necessary, and practice good hygiene.

- To maintain a high level of energy, consume plenty of water and wholesome foods. Discover classic British holiday fare while balancing it with a range of other foods for a balanced diet.

- Schedule your day's activities while leaving time for downtime. To enjoy the celebrations, try to avoid overdoing it.

- Pay attention to your possessions, particularly in busy areas. Be aware of pickpockets, in well-known tourist areas, and keep your belongings safe.

- Pick lodgings with an excellent reputation for cleanliness and safety. To make an educated decision, do some preliminary research and read reviews.

- Pay close attention to public transportation safety regulations. When boarding trains or buses, pay attention to the space and take caution when using escalators and stairs.

- To keep safe, follow traffic laws while crossing roads, utilize authorized crosswalks, and pay attention to your surroundings.

- Save crucial phone numbers, such as those for the emergency services, your embassy, or your consulate. It's important to know who to call in an emergency.

- Be respectful and nice to workers, residents, and other tourists. A happy outlook will improve your vacation interactions and experiences.

- If you're feeling stressed out, take a break and locate a quiet place to unwind. Manage stress by engaging in enjoyable activities, such as going for a walk in the park or relaxing with a hot coffee in a comfortable café.

- Don't be afraid to see a doctor or go to a healthcare institution if you have health issues or require medical guidance.

You will guarantee a peaceful and happy Christmas break in London by heeding these simple safety and health recommendations. Put your health first if you want to create enduring memories this holiday season.

Stay Safe and Sound: Emergency Contacts in Festive London

Knowing who to contact in case of any unforeseen circumstances during your Christmas journey in London is crucial. Here are important emergency numbers and details to keep you safe:

- **Emergency Services:**

Dial 999 for immediate police assistance in emergencies or to report a crime. Dial 999 if you need fire or rescue services. Dial 999 for medical emergencies and ambulance services.

- **Non-Emergency Police:**

Use this non-emergency police number 101 to report incidents that don't require immediate response.

- **National Health Service (NHS):**

Dial 111 for medical advice and assistance for non-life-threatening situations.

- **Local Medical Facilities:**

Know the nearest hospital in your area. Hospitals in London have emergency departments to handle urgent medical needs.

- **Embassy or Consulate:**

Keep the contact details of your country's embassy or consulate for assistance or emergencies related to your nationality.

- **Lost or Stolen Items:**

If you lose something, contact the relevant lost property office. For London Transport, visit their website or contact TFL. Contact the local police to report stolen belongings.

- **Tourist Information Centers:**

VisitBritain Tourist Information: 020 7578 1400 for general tourist information and assistance.

Local Tourist Centers: Located throughout the city, providing information and guidance.

Friendly Locals or Staff:

If you need immediate assistance or directions, don't hesitate to approach friendly locals or service staff.

Keeping these emergency contacts handy on your phone or in a safe spot will give you peace of mind during your festive journey through London. Stay safe, be prepared, and enjoy the holiday season.

Framing the Joy: Picture-Perfect Moments in London during Christmas

It's a great way to keep memories alive to capture the beauty of Christmas in London with your camera. Here are some suggestions to make sure your holiday photo book is filled with stunning, picture-perfect shots:

- Identify prominent London locations that are recognized for their holiday charm and Christmas decorations before you go.

- Take use of the gentle, warm light during the golden hours just after dawn and before sunset to give your photographs a magical feel.

- To capture the festive mood, frame your photographs to incorporate Christmas trees, decorations, and jovial people.

- Photograph people having fun at the celebrations; candid photos often convey a more sincere and endearing narrative.

- To highlight the beauty of the season, concentrate on the minute details of the ornaments, lights, and decorations.

- Mix things up by snapping pictures from high angles to capture the energy of the crowd or low angles for a new viewpoint.

- For a spectacular effect, photograph the reflections of Christmas lights on damp sidewalks or storefront windows.

- Take group or individual photographs of your friends and family in front of holiday decorations or well-known London landmarks.

- Use a quick shutter speed to record people riding rides at Christmas markets or ice skating on rinks.

- When taking night photos, experiment with longer exposure times to catch the city's sparkling lights and produce lovely light trails.

- Use editing apps sparingly and carefully. After taking the photo, utilize easy editing software to improve the colors, contrast, and brightness. But keep in mind, sometimes less is more.

- Enjoy the Process by being present. While it's nice to record memories, don't forget to enjoy the Christmas season by getting lost in the celebration.

Keep in mind that the goal of photography is to capture the excitement and spirit of the occasion. Enjoy every click, and use them to create a visual tale of London's enchanted Christmas moments.

Making Lasting Memories: Taking in the Best of Christmas Time in London

The key to making amazing Christmastime experiences in London is to immerse yourself in the enchanted setting and participate in the celebrations.

- Peruse the quaint Christmas markets, savoring the holiday spirit and maybe discovering one-of-a-kind treasures.

- Glide on the ice while surrounded by bright lights and upbeat music at renowned rinks like Somerset House or the Natural History Museum.

- Take pleasure in holiday lights, especially Christmas illuminations. Take a walk around Oxford Street or Carnaby Street at night to see the city lit up in imaginative and stunning ways.

- Take in some theater magic by seeing a holiday performance. With your loved ones, attend a joyous ballet performance or a touching Christmas play.

- Visit Santa's Grotto and see Father Christmas, among other things. Bring the kids to see Santa Claus and his elves in one of the charming grottos scattered across the city.

- Indulge in classic mince pies, roasted chestnuts, or rich hot chocolate from tiny London cafés to treat your taste buds.

- Participate in a carol service and sing along to carols. Attend a carol performance at a stunning church in London and participate in the singing of your favorite holiday songs.

- Adore the Trafalgar Square Tree. Admire the magnificent Christmas tree that Norway has donated as a sign of friendliness and holiday cheer.

- Explore lesser-known streets to find equally spectacular hidden decorations and quaint nooks.

- Get aboard a festively decked-out bus tour to see London's Christmas splendor from a different angle.

- Get Crafty and participate in seminars where you will be able to make your holiday decorations or ornaments.

- Participate in local Christmas cheer-raising activities like tree lightings and charity drives.

- Share the joy and capture the moment. Create a photo book with your friends and family and take a lot of pictures to remember these special moments in the future.

In London, where there are holiday surprises around every turn, embrace the holiday mood. Keep these memories close to your heart since they are what make this season unique.

London's Christmas spirit paints a narrative of love, joy, and community right in the center of the busy metropolis. A song of festive joy is created by the sparkling lights, the brisk winter air, and the laughing that reverberates through the streets. Let's go back on the lovely memories and experiences this wonderful season gives to those who embrace it as we draw to a close with this Christmas travel guide.

Christmas in London is much more than simply the opulent sights and brilliant lights. It's about the smiles that are exchanged, the pleasant interactions with strangers, and the sense of community in a city that is welcoming to everybody at this particular moment. It's the fulfillment of giving and receiving, of making precious memories with close friends and family. Every second of this holiday season, from ice skating under the stars and drinking hot chocolate by the fire, leaves a mark on the canvas of our memories. What makes the

Christmas season special are the everyday joys of browsing the markets, listening to carolers, and enjoying seasonal goodies. In the end, it's the small things that stick with us; the shared giggles over a cup of mulled wine, the wonder in a child's eyes as they encounter Santa Claus, and the quiet looks that express our happiness. It's about appreciating the wonder of Christmas, experiencing the love all around us, and being in the moment.

Let your emotions be your guide as you explore London's bright winter wonderland throughout the holidays. Keep each moment in mind since it is these little intervals of time that give our lives its depth and beauty. Let the merry music and jingly lights fill your spirit, and may the holiday cheer follow you long after the final ornament is taken down. I hope your Christmas is full of joy, love, and the warmth of cherished memories.

Happy Holidays!

Made in the USA
Las Vegas, NV
18 November 2024